50 Ways to Love Your Retirement

Approaching the Heart with a Rational Mind

Sarah Cline, Ph.D.

Copyright © 2023 Sarah Cline, Ph.D.

All rights reserved.

The contents of this book may not be reproduced, duplicated, or transmitted without direct written permission from the author.

Under no circumstances will any legal responsibility or blame be held against the publisher for any reparation, damages, or monetary loss due to the information herein, either directly or indirectly.

Legal Notice:

This book is copyright-protected. This is only for personal use. You cannot amend, distribute, sell, use, quote, or paraphrase any part of the content within this book without the consent of the author.

Disclaimer Notice:

Please note the information contained within this document is for educational and entertainment purposes only. Every attempt has been made to provide accurate, up-to-date, and reliable complete information. No warranties of any kind are expressed or implied. Readers acknowledge that the author is not engaging in the rendering of legal, financial, medical, or professional advice. The content of this book has been derived from various sources. Please consult a licensed professional before attempting any techniques outlined in this book.

By reading this document, the reader agrees that under no circumstances is the author responsible for any losses, direct or indirect, which are incurred as a result of the use of the information contained within this document, including, but not limited to, errors, omissions, or inaccuracies.

Contents

1. Introduction — 1
2. Understanding Personality Types: A Deep Dive — 3
3. Communicate Your Retirement — 17
4. Embrace a New Identity — 39
5. Celebrate Your Past — 57
6. Celebrate Your Present — 69
7. Don't Forget Your Finances — 80
8. Keep Yourself Busy — 89
9. Final Thoughts — 115
10. Appendices — 119

Chapter One

Introduction

Retirement can be fun and exciting. However, it can also be complex and often shrouded in guilt or fear of the unknown—so much so that it may be difficult to enjoy at times. But fear not, dear reader. By merely picking up this book, you are taking a brave first step toward understanding and enhancing your retirement.

Within these pages, we'll delve into three distinct personality types: the reserved Cave Dweller (CD), the outgoing Mountain Yeller (MY), and the Straddler, who exhibit traits from both categories. With practical insights and real-life examples of these personality types, you'll have an arsenal at your disposal to help you navigate the intricate dynamics of relationships while also gaining a deeper understanding of yourself. After all, your relationships are critical to enjoying retirement, and learning about how to grow, develop, or maintain them is critical to your long-term success.

Ahead, we will learn about the different personality types, and at the end of the book, you will be able to take a test to determine which type you most closely relate to! If you find yourself needing to grow emotionally closer to someone—or even just understand them a little better—consider giving them the quiz, too.

Learning about Personality Types

Buckle up; we're about to uncover the mysteries of CDs, MYs, and Straddlers. Think of it as a personality safari where we'll observe these fascinating creatures in their natural habitat and gain a deeper understanding of each type. Then we'll explore how they might pertain to your everyday life. Armed with this knowledge, you'll be able to decode behaviors and avoid misinterpretations like a pro. No more of the blame game when it comes to misunderstandings; it's all about recognizing and respecting our inherent differences. So, let's hop on this wild ride and learn how to better appreciate your retirement for what it is and what it can be.

First Thing First

Forget the quick fixes and checklists; loving others is an active effort. This book will guide you, but it's up to you to truly apply these insights. It may require some soul-searching and challenging your current beliefs, but the payoff is worth it— a deeper bond and a better understanding of yourself and those you love and the key to unlocking true happiness in retirement.

Chapter Two

Understanding Personality Types: A Deep Dive

Do you need help to understand the personality traits of your family or friends? What about yourself?

Understanding personality types is an essential piece of the puzzle when seeking to understand others and yourself. Appreciating people (and yourself) means discovering one's true layers and complexities.

In this chapter, we will discuss the personality types of the Cave Dweller, which we will refer to as CD, the Mountain Yeller or MY, and the Straddler. Learning about these three basic personality types will give you a clearer picture of the unique benefits and challenges each creates. Understanding that is an essential first step to bringing harmony and happiness into your retirement.

Origins of Personality Types

Before the modern-day classifications of CDs and Mys, and even before psychiatrists and psychologists stepped onto the scene, ancient civilizations sought to explain human behavior and its various nuances.

The Ancient Greeks

The ancient Greeks developed the theory of "four humors" to explain the causes of health and illness, both mental and physical. This theory suggested that an individual's temperament was influenced by bodily fluids: blood (sanguine), yellow bile (choleric), black bile (melancholic), and phlegm (phlegmatic). The Greeks thought these humors were directly related to being sanguine (cheerful), choleric (short-tempered), melancholic (reserved), or phlegmatic (relaxed). Therefore, the balance of these humors was believed to influence an individual's temperament, health, and overall disposition. An imbalance of this humor led to behaviors that we associate with certain mental illnesses today. For example:

- Sanguine (blood) was associated with cheerful, optimistic, enthusiastic personality traits. An imbalance was thought to be due to a person having too much blood in their body, which would cause them to be overly confident and have impulsive behavior. Possible narcissistic and bipolar disorder.

- Choleric (yellow bile) was associated with being ambitious, passionate, and easily angered. An imbalance causes anger, irritability, or extremely aggressive behavior and rage. Possible borderline personality disorder.

- Melancholic (black bile) was associated with being thoughtful, reflective, and often sad or depressed. This imbalance was associated with melancholy and depression.

- Phlegmatic (phlegm) was associated with being calm, reliable, and often unemotional or apathetic. An imbalance was associated with lethargy, sluggishness, or a lack of motivation, which, much like melancholic, is a symptom of depression.

Treating these emotional ailments is where things got even more interesting. If the Greeks thought you had an imbalance of any of these four humors, you would likely have received one of the following treatments:

- **Dietary Changes:** Prescribed depending on the humor in excess. For instance, someone deemed overly choleric might be advised to avoid hot or spicy foods that would "agitate" the yellow bile.

- **Bloodletting:** If you were someone believed to have an excess of sanguine humor, it was common practice to be prescribed bloodletting. This process involved removing blood from the body by way of leeches or actual cutting.

- **Purging:** To remove excess bile or phlegm, laxatives were used, as were emetics, which induced vomiting.

- **Baths/Sweating:** To promote toxin removal, balms and ointments were applied to the skin to help imbalance these four humors.

The Greeks' attempts to "treat" imbalances in personality or health were based on the observations and knowledge they had at the time. The four humors theory was eventually replaced with more accurate medical models, but their influence can still be seen in some of our languages today.

The Introvert and the Extrovert

Carl Gustav Jung (1875–1961) was a Swiss psychiatrist, psychoanalyst, and the father of analytical psychology. He developed several concepts that had a profound influence on both psychology and popular culture. One of his most notable contributions was the concept of *introversion* and *extraversion* (often used in the more modern manner: *introvert* and *extrovert*). Jung's theory asserts that introversion and extraversion are attitudes that represent the direction in which a person's psychic energy flows.

Extraversion (Extrovert)

According to Jung, the extrovert's energy flows outward. This personality type is more oriented toward the external world and derives energy from interacting with its surroundings, including people, events, and situations. If someone is an extrovert, they tend to be more outgoing, social, and interested in external events. They are typically action-oriented and more comfortable in social situations than an introverted person. External factors influence extroverts, who are occasionally prone to negative introspection.

Introversion (Introvert)

As the name suggests, the introvert's energy flows inward. This personality type is more oriented toward their inner world, relying on introspection and internal reflection. If someone is introverted, they are generally more reserved and often feel more comfortable with individual activities or smaller group settings. They derive energy and pleasure from thinking, daydreaming, or exploring ideas. Although an introverted person's daily practices tend to lead to social isolation, they tend to have a small number of deep connections with people of their choosing.

Jung believed that everyone has an introverted and extroverted side, with one being more dominant than the other. It's a spectrum, and while some might be near the extremes of that spectrum, most individuals lie somewhere in between.

Cave Dweller (CD) and Mountain Yeller (MY)

While our contemporary understanding of the CD and MY classifications doesn't stem directly from ancient Greek or Jungian theories, much like their historical counterparts, they are observed patterns in modern relationships. By identifying recurring patterns, we can forge tools to help us navigate and harmonize interpersonal interactions.

Cave Dweller (CD)

We must first learn about their traits to determine where you and your loved ones fall on the spectrum of CD to MY.

Reserved Nature

If someone is a CD, they will predominantly be calm and reserved. CDs are introspective and tend to hold their emotions close to their chest because they value their inner world and the sanctuary it provides. Their reserved nature doesn't mean that they are indifferent or don't care about those around them; it just means that they process their emotions internally and over time. For instance, after an argument, a CD might withdraw to process their feelings rather than immediately confront an issue. A CD does this because they typically feel uncomfortable with strife and need time to work through their emotions and decide how to communicate their feelings.

Socially, a CD is often found in quieter corners engaging in deep conversation with one or two individuals rather than in the center of a party. In group discussions, a CD will offer insights only if specifically asked or if they feel strongly about a topic.

Logical Thinking and Literal Communication

A CD leans more toward analytical and logical thinking. They make decisions only after careful contemplation and weighing the pros and cons. They work hard to keep their emotions from clouding their judgment. This logical thinking manifests in their communication; they will get to the point without inserting emotions or using stories to embellish their point.

For example, if you discuss a film with a CD, they will likely dissect plot points with impeccable logic and even point out strengths and weaknesses; but they often miss the emotional undertones of the movie. If you ask a CD if they liked the cake you brought for dessert, they might reply "Yes" without diving into flowery descriptives.

It's important to note that a CD may also get frustrated with an embellished story that takes longer to get to the point. It doesn't mean they don't want to hear the story or don't care what you have to say; their brain is just geared toward immediate outcomes.

Need for Space

A CD has an inherent need for emotional and physical personal space. For them, requiring space is not about distancing themselves from loved ones. It's about needing solitude to recharge and reflect.

CDs enjoy reading books in a cozy nook or going for solitary walks. They may listen to music while cooking dinner instead of talking. This alone time is essential for a CD, especially after a day filled with social interactions.

Singular Focus

A CD has unparalleled concentration when engrossed in a task and prefers completing that task to their satisfaction before tackling another.

If you attempt to talk to a CD while they're writing an email, for example, they may be so absorbed in what they're writing that you'll be tuned out. It's not that what you're saying is unimportant to them; it's just challenging for them to extend focus to more than one thing at a time because they give each item their full attention.

Social Preferences

Traditionally, if someone was labeled an introvert, others would consider them anti-social. But that couldn't be farther from the truth. An introvert, or a CD, just leans toward more intimate social interactions. Large gatherings can overwhelm a CD and drain their mental and emotional battery.

Emotional Processing

While CDs might not outwardly express their emotions, they experience them deeply. However, their internal reflections may lead to a delay in their outward emotional expression. While a CD may seem distant after an emotional confrontation, they must process the interaction before reacting. A CD needs time to contemplate a disagreement, analyze the conversation, and figure out where things went wrong before they can move on to a resolution. This meditation is essential for a CD's family member to understand. The more you push them to express themselves, the more they will clam up in response.

Deeper Dive into the Mountain Yeller (MY)

If someone is an extrovert, chances are they've been called that more than once in their lifetime. An extrovert is typically known for being outgoing and the life of any party. But there's so much more to them than meets the eye.

Outgoing Nature/Group Socialization

An MY is inherently outgoing. Their energy thrives on interactions and being around people as often as possible. Instead of needing time alone to recharge, MYs wants to be out and involved.

At a social event, MYs are the first to initiate games and dancing. They often bounce from person to person catching up rather than focusing on one task at a time. Deep conversations are still on the table, but not at a social event. An MY usually rallies their friends for a group outing over a weekend rather than sitting at home reading a book or watching TV. In the workplace, MYs love group projects and find collaborative brainstorming and teamwork exciting.

Emotion-Driven

MYs are heart-ruled because they lead with their intuition and emotions. Being ruled by their heart doesn't mean their decisions are devoid of logic, but their feelings heavily influence their reactions. An MY can be emotional during arguments but is also the first to send a heartfelt message to a friend or family member upon hearing they are having a rough time.

MY emotions show throughout their storytelling, so be patient when they tell you about an event or relay the plot to a movie. Chances are both will be full of details and embellishments.

Connection and Touch

MYs crave genuine connections and physical touch, whether a hug, a pat on the back, or simply holding hands. It reinforces their feeling of being connected. In relating with you, an MY will crave physical affection and see it as a top priority over other needs—something we'll discuss in depth a bit later.

Dynamic Focus

An MY is a natural multitasker. Instead of focusing on one task at a time, their attention shifts between assignments. They enjoy the energy they get from juggling multiple things and often get bored working on one project for an extended period.

An MY doesn't mind dealing with paperwork but works through it while watching television or listening to music. As for conversations, an MY loves to chat, but don't be surprised if you find them scrolling on their phone while talking with you. It's not that they think what you have to say is unimportant; their mind simply just runs at a faster rate than a CD, making them more comfortable processing more than one thing at a time.

Inferential Communication

An MY often communicates using stories, anecdotes, and metaphors rather than getting straight to the point. They rely on indirect implications and expect others to infer meaning, which can confuse some who aren't familiar with their communication style.

During an argument, someone may find it hard to decipher what the MY really wants, even if the MY feels they have expressed it directly. It's essential to have a middle ground where communication is concerned, especially if your loved one is an MY and you are a CD.

Immediate Emotional Expression

Unlike their CD counterparts, MYs are quick to express their emotions. They're an open book and rarely hesitate to share their feelings of joy and disappointment. This can be overwhelming for a CD uncomfortable with an emotional display.

One of the greatest fears an MY faces is the fear of rejection. If an MY has a CD child who usually pulls away at any sign of conflict, this can be a bone of contention. An MY will take your withdrawal as a sign of personal rejection. It's important to communicate that you are not rejecting them and need time to wrap your head around and process the disagreement. Give the MY verbal and physical affirmations whenever possible.

If you are a CD and your loved one is an MY, don't panic; it doesn't mean you cannot have a successful relationship. There are plenty of amazing and fulfilling relationships between opposites. It just takes time, work, and patience to learn one another's needs and effectively communicate.

The Straddler

If your loved ones (or you) are a Straddler, they (or you) are adaptable and enjoy the best of both worlds. They can immerse themselves in a book like a CD or be the life of a party like an MY. They possess an emotional agility that allows them to straddle their personality types seamlessly. While this book predominantly focuses on CD and MY, Straddlers can use it to understand the extremes and navigate their middle ground more effectively.

Balance Between Reflection and Expression

A Straddler can introspect like a CD, valuing quiet moments of thought. Yet, they also appreciate the expressive vitality that an MY has, and they can share their feelings and ideas openly when a situation calls for it. They are as happy spending a quiet evening reading or attending a book club as they are actively participating in a lively discussion.

Adaptable in Social Situations

While they might not always be the life of the party, Straddlers easily adjust to situations based on the social settings and the company involved. They can engage in a one-on-one conversation at a party and then join a group game or be at the party's center later in the evening.

Values Both Logic and Emotion

A Straddler approaches situations with a logical mindset but is equally attuned to the emotional undercurrents, valuing the importance of feelings in decision-making. For example, if a colleague faces a personal issue, the Straddler will offer practical solutions while providing emotional support.

Flexibility in Needs and Fears

The Straddler's hierarchy of needs fluctuates based on circumstances, and they might experience the fears of a CD, such as loss of security, and the MY's fear of rejection. However, adaptability allows them to prioritize different aspects of their life. While working on an important business project, they will prioritize career stability, but in downtime, they will focus on relationships and personal connections.

Fluid Communication Styles

A Straddler can communicate directly and inferentially, often adjusting communication based on the recipient. For example, when conversing with an analytical boss, they will be direct and to the point, but when they talk to their best friend, they become expressive and delve into all the nitty-gritty details.

Straddlers possess an innate ability to mediate and find common ground, especially in relationships where CDs and MYs might find themselves at odds. Their adaptability enables them to comprehend and empathize with both personality types, easing communication and diminishing misunderstandings.

A Straddler may seem like the perfect personality type. However, everyone encounters their share of struggles. The Straddler's flexibility can confuse their preferences and needs. The Straddler might sometimes feel stretched or trapped in the middle, particularly in a polarized situation where they wish to please others so much that they struggle to voice their disagreements. A Straddler must discern what is truly significant to them while learning to navigate other personality types, much like everyone else.

So, How Do You Find Common Ground?

The good news is that this book doesn't tell you how to "cope" with differences; it allows you the opportunity to realize each person's unique strengths in a relationship. A CD's introspection can balance an MY's spontaneity. An MY's vivacity and exuberance can harmonize beautifully with a CD's depth and stability.

Recognizing these different traits is merely the first step to a healthy relationship. The real challenge, and indeed the focus of this book, is to find ways to navigate the complexities of these interactions and how they relate to your retirement. The beauty of a relationship truly unfolds in the dance between these personalities, and your retirement is a great opportunity to grow and develop relationships both past and new.

Key Takeaways

Diving into the intricacies of personality types isn't about affixing labels but enriching our understanding. With these insights, you're now armed with the necessary vocabulary to navigate the labyrinth of human emotions and connections, fostering an environment where love thrives, understanding blossoms, and relationships flourish. As we traverse this journey, let's remember that the goal isn't to change but to adapt, understand, and love more deeply.

The foundation for a nurturing relationship starts with understanding—understanding yourself and your loved ones and the dynamics of your interaction with one another. With the knowledge of CD and MY personality traits, you're well on your way to deepening that understanding, setting the stage for the subsequent chapters that will guide you on how to cherish your loved ones in ways that resonate with all of you.

Understanding personality differences is essential for nurturing compatibility. This chapter has illuminated the fundamental traits of CDs, MYs, and Straddlers.

- **Reserved Nature:** Respect your CD loved one's need for personal space and quiet reflection. Don't force immediate emotional reactions.

- **Logical Thinking:** Recognize your CD loved one's analytical approach. Be patient as they process before expressing feelings.

- **Singular Focus**: Acknowledge that multitasking is difficult for your CD loved ones. Allow them to complete or pause their task before they give you their full attention.

- **Emotion-Driven:** Empathize with your MY loved one's emotions. Give them positive affirmations/compliments and physical affection.

- **Inferential Communication:** Listen for meanings implied indirectly in your MY loved one's stories. Learn to read between the lines.

- **Dynamic Focus**: Accept your MY loved one's wandering attention. Multitasking is in their nature. However, if you need their full focus, tell them.

- **Excellent Balance:** Appreciate the adaptability of a Straddler, but avoid putting them in the middle of conflicts.

- **Flexible Needs:** Accommodate shifts in a Straddler's priorities. Reassure them of your unconditional love.

Chapter Three

Communicate Your Retirement

Retirement marks a significant transition in life, and it seems to be like a shiny penny in the street, brimming with exciting possibilities as well as intricate challenges. This chapter is dedicated to understanding the crucial role communication plays in this phase of your life. Beyond financial planning, it emphasizes the importance of open dialogue within your family, employer, and especially with your spouse. From expressing your desires to navigating family dynamics and setting clear boundaries, effective communication is the cornerstone for a smooth and fulfilling retirement journey. This chapter guides you through the art of discussing your retirement plans, addressing concerns, and creating a shared understanding that paves the way for a harmonious retired life.

Express Feelings on Your Readiness to Retire

While it is entirely possible to retire without having a conversation with your family members, we recommend you discuss the plan with a few of those close to you. If you're married, your partner needs to be included in the decision, and if you aren't married, it still might be a good idea to discuss your intention to retire with some members of your family.

Making decisions about your retirement is no small task. These sorts of decisions include where you want to live, how you might protect your assets, sustain your lifestyle, or even what kind of help you may need as you journey through the rest of your life. Speaking with your family about these decisions can make them easier.

Remember, as you make it further into retirement, it is entirely possible that things may change, such as the arrival of new grandchildren, the state of your health, etc. You want to make sure that you can communicate potential solutions to any changes you can foresee and ask (and allow others to ask) those tough "what ifs." Brainstorming parties can help with this!

Of course, discussing retirement plans with family members is not always an easy task. There are family dynamics, communication styles, and other factors that may make it even more difficult to share pertinent information with others.

For example, it's entirely possible your adult child is not ready to talk about you moving or planning for end-of-life care. Discuss it briefly and take their feelings into consideration. However, do make sure that you revisit the conversation when they're ready, or at the very least do some estate planning.

Avoid Confusion

Sharing retirement plans with family allows everyone the opportunity to ask questions, voice concerns, and explain their points of view. Getting your family on board with your plans will avoid confusion and alleviate disagreements if a situation occurs that requires their aid. For example, make sure you discuss scenarios where you might become dependent on them for care.

Although everything is ultimately up to you, don't forget that your loved ones may have valuable input that could help you finalize your decisions. It may be difficult to hear some feedback, especially if it doesn't align with your ideas, but make sure that you give everyone the chance to speak. This will alleviate the potential for more issues down the road and can give everyone peace of mind.

What to Discuss When You Share Your Plans

Make sure you discuss your boundaries. Just because you have more free time doesn't necessarily mean you have time to do extra things they may want from you. Keep in mind how much time you're willing to spend on others.

Also, make sure that you discuss if you're planning on moving to a senior living community now or in the future. Determine what kind of care or support you need and a timeline in which you may need it. It may even be a good idea to discuss Power of Attorney options since that is often an important aspect of retirement.

- **Health Status**: Give your family a realistic idea about your current state of health. Ask for their input while you share any diagnoses you have. It's especially important to disclose hereditary health conditions.

- **Living Arrangements:** If you're sharing your decision to move to a retirement community with your family, let them know a timeframe and discuss the facility you're planning to move into. Consider their feelings if this is a plan occurring particularly soon.

- **Future Care Wishes:** Discuss with your spouse and children, if you have them how you wish to be cared for in the event of a serious health crisis. It's important to appoint someone with a longer life expectancy than you to fulfill these wishes. An attorney can help with this, but make sure you talk to your loved ones first. Be sure to approach the topic with empathy and care. Remember, just because you've thought a lot about this doesn't mean that they have. This would be a good time to jot down feedback and have an attorney help you turn decisions into reality.

Although your family's feedback is important, remember that you call the final shots. If you want your plans set in stone prior to your conversation with them, that is your prerogative. However, expect feedback regardless.

Tips for a Successful Conversation

When preparing to talk about your retirement plans with your family, it is important to note that not everyone uses the same communication styles. It's important to remember that:

- **You don't need to share everything at once.** If sharing your news about health or plans to move to a retirement community or just another location is overwhelming to your loved ones, you may want to wait until they've processed some to talk about the rest.

- **It's important to be patient.** Your children and loved ones may not be as ready as you are to talk about your plans, especially those that might deal with your mortality. Respect their emotions and set the pace for a productive discussion.

- **You can plan ahead.** Waiting for the perfect time to share might keep you waiting longer than you want. Plan when and where you'll discuss this information, and be sure everyone who needs to be there is there.

- **You should always be honest.** Give simple explanations as to why you made the decisions that you've made. You can choose how open you are, but be honest. Share your true desires and concerns openly, and allow your family to see the situation from your point of view.

- **It's OK to ask for help.** If you need to, find a third party to help you facilitate this discussion with your family members. Your doctor, care manager, or elder law attorney can offer consulting services, which may be helpful in the case of complicated family relationships.

Use Neutral Language to Curb Defensiveness

Your choice of words significantly impacts the tone of your communication with your family at any given time. To prevent defensiveness and promote understanding, avoid accusatory language if disagreements arise; instead, focus on the specific behavior or issue. Accusations will lead your family members to focus more on defending themselves rather than understanding you or your perspective. That is not a desired goal here (or during any conversation). Instead, discuss how *you feel*.

Use "We" Statements

Using "we" instead of "you" statements conveys that you are all in this together, working as a team to resolve a problem. Relationships are a two-way street, so what better way to show that you're trying to expand your relationship? It is important to communicate that you are practicing empathy as well as acknowledging their feelings and perspectives. This is your retirement, but as you communicate, try to incorporate "we" statements as often as possible, even if the primary focus is on you specifically.

Don't Say This

"You never understand where I'm coming from." This is a generalization. They may know where you're coming from at times, and saying otherwise is a good way to halt the conversation from desired outcomes, especially if this is your spouse. This puts an immediate negative connotation on the conversation and puts them into defensive mode.

Instead, Say This

"We seem to have a disconnect sometimes in our communication." Emphasizing "we" makes the conversation more about finding solutions together rather than pointing fingers, which can often lead to a more productive and less confrontational discussion. Whatever hurdle you need to get through in your discussion, it can't be overcome if your loved one feels like they have to defend themselves.

Use "I" Statements

Expressing yourself without becoming overly aggressive can be challenging when faced with a conflict, especially if you feel your loved one is pushing buttons. To avoid underhandedness at this time and help de-escalate the situation and clarify your point, an "I" or an assertive statement is an effective psychiatrist-approved approach.

Don't Say This

"You are always trying to tell me what to do." Again, this is a generalization and carries a negative connotation.

Instead, Say This

"I feel a little overwhelmed when you assert your opinion in that way." This "I" statement expresses your feelings and your need for them to stop asserting their opinion in a way that is upsetting you—without blaming or accusing them. After all, if you're having this conversation with them, it's likely because their input does matter to a degree. Make sure you're hearing what they're saying, but both of you need to understand that you will have different perspectives. It's about how you come up with a solution that matters. Do this respectfully, and if you need time, take a breather! Come back to the conversation later.

Don't Say This

"You never listen to me." This is also a generalization.

Instead, Say This

"I feel frustrated when I feel unheard. I would like it if we worked on listening to each other a little more effectively." This type of communication makes it so that each of you has something to work on. After all, we all could use a little extra help in effective communication and active listening.

Speaking this way also avoids tactics of attack, critique, and criticism, which usually lead to more hostility and defensiveness. In general, using "I" messages can create a constructive dialogue about the true causes of any conflict by avoiding aggressive behaviors and fostering effective communication.

Listen to Your Family's Feedback

Practice active listening when others communicate with you. Avoid interrupting them when they're speaking, even if you disagree. Active listening is the cornerstone of all effective communication. It involves not only hearing the words they say but understanding their emotions and perspectives. Validate them and show them that you're listening by maintaining eye contact and providing non-verbal cues like nodding. Our body language matters. Be present in the conversation and take their feelings and criticisms seriously. Don't be distracted by external forces. Never multitask while someone is communicating with you. Listen to and reflect on what they are saying before responding. Be sure to ask open-ended questions to encourage them to share more, and remember one thing: if they are communicating it, it's important.

Here are a few important discussion points to include.

- **Where important papers are:** Tell someone you know and trust, or a lawyer, where to find your important papers. Hopefully, now that you're going into retirement, you've completed them. Discuss this with your family: who knows what information, etc. You don't need to discuss your personal affairs, but someone you trust should know where to find your papers in case of an emergency, and your family members should know who this person is.

- **Healthcare plans go a long way:** A doctor can, of course, help you understand your health status, which can in turn help you in making health decisions. They are generally great at helping you make plans for the kinds of care of treatment you might need or can expect. Discussing advanced-care planning with your doctor is free through Medicare during your annual wellness visit. Private health insurance may also cover these sorts of discussions. Share these conversations with your loved ones to help avoid surprises or misunderstandings about your health or the wishes you have for your care in the future. Give permission in advance for a doctor or lawyer to talk with who you appoint as a caregiver or Power of Attorney. If you need help managing your care, you can give your caregiver permission to talk with your doctors, lawyer, insurance provider, credit card company, or bank. Consult your lawyer to find the best solutions for you and your family, but know that keeping everyone in the loop on health decisions will go a long way and will set you up for success in retirement without pesky surprises.

- **Reviewing your plans regularly is important**: It's important to review your plans at least once each year or when any major life event occurs, like a divorce, move, or major change in your health.

- **Legal preparations**: You may want to talk with a lawyer about setting up a general power of attorney, durable power of attorney, joint account, or trust. Be sure to ask about the lawyer's fees before you make an appointment.

Other decisions you can prepare in advance include:

- Funeral arrangements
- DNR (Do Not Resuscitate order)
- Organ donation

Make that you're communicating all of this to your family and listening to their feedback on each topic.

Communicate with Your Lawyer, Accountant, or Financial Advisor

Getting your affairs in order can be daunting, but with the proper professionals in place, it can be a whole lot easier. Make sure that you draft different types of legal documents that outline how your estate and finances will be handled. Common documents include a will, durable power of attorney for finances, and a living trust.

- **Will:** Your will decrees how your property, money, and other assets will be distributed and managed when you die. A will can also be used to address the care for children under age 18, adult dependents, and pets, as well as end-of-life arrangements such as a funeral or memorial service and burial or cremation. If you do not have a will, your estate will be distributed according to the laws in your state.

- **Durable power of attorney:** A durable power of attorney for finances names someone who will make financial decisions for you when you are unable to. You should also have a POA for medical needs.

- **Living trust**: A living trust names and instructs a person known as the trustee to hold and distribute property and funds on your behalf when you are no longer able to manage your affairs.

Communicate with Your Employer

Obviously, it's common courtesy to let your employer know your retirement plans. It's important to communicate with them your desire and your plans as early as you know them. They can help you get your work affairs planned out and in place before it's time. They may even know about extra benefits that you may not realize you have earned by working there.

Your boss can typically arrange for you to train the next person in line to take your place and work as an advocate in many situations to get your retirement off on the right foot. Also, when it's finally time to leave work, don't forget to send them a letter of thanks or what is known as a retirement message. This is important because it not only leaves everyone engaged and happy with your departure but also leaves a door open if there is ever a reason you need to come back.

To write such a note for your boss or colleagues, make sure to keep the tone lighthearted. Remember, it's OK to be excited for the next chapter. You have worked hard over the course of your career, and you deserve the chance to take a step back and spend more time with your loved ones.

That doesn't necessarily mean everyone is excited to see you go. You may be writing a farewell message to people you've worked with for many years, and like it or not, your relationships will be changing.

Communicate the New Boundaries Your Retirement Will Bring

With your retirement comes a lot of changes. Communicating boundaries with your loved ones is essential for a happy retirement! For example, you don't want your kids to think that you have all the time in the world to babysit your grandkids if you plan on doing something else with your time. You may not want people just dropping in or calling all hours of the day. Make sure you're having conversations with loved ones regarding your wants and needs during this time.

Communicate Directly with Your Spouse

Making the leap to retirement can be challenging enough for one person alone, but married couples tend to face other unique challenges when it comes to these changes to their lives and the relationship in general.

Think about it: all of a sudden, your spouse is home far more, and you have to navigate them and all of their quirks all day every day. These quirks can turn into problems quickly. Even happily married couples face a little friction from time to time. It's important that you communicate your expectations to one another.

Boundaries help spouses prioritize their needs as individuals and as a couple so both of you can feel confident and excited about retirement.

Remember, your spouse can't read your mind—even if you think they can.

They didn't intuitively know that leaving the toothbrush sitting on the bathroom counter irritated you when you first got married, and they won't know how you want to spend retirement if you don't tell them.

Many couples are surprised to learn that they have different ideas about their ideal retirement. Of course, if you are happily married, it is only natural that you can't wait to retire! Think of all the wonderful things you can do with your spouse with extra time on your hands! You can travel to all those destinations and do all the things that seemed impossible when you were working or raising children.

Congratulations!

However, it is important to recognize that you and your spouse may have different visions and that the two of you need to communicate what those visions are. One of you may be excited to relax and play golf. You may want to take long lunches, still work part-time, and spend more time with family. However, the other may want to fulfill all those travel bucket lists and spend more time abroad than with family. You need to align your visions and build one that is fulfilling for each person. This is where those personality traits come into play. Understanding whether you and your spouse are MYs, CDs, or Straddlers can help the two of you align your visions more appropriately and find the perfect balance to keep everyone happy and energized.

Walk through these questions with your spouse.

- What's your vision for our retirement?
- What excites you most about that plan?
- Where do you see me fitting into that vision?

It's critical to note that there's a massive difference between vision and reality. While one of you may think a beach retirement may sound like a real dream in theory, in practice you may not like all the sand and the tourists. Maybe you burn easily or are too far away from family and friends. Discuss these things with each other and what you can see the two of you doing.

Carve Space for Individual Goals and Pursuits

As a married couple, you're likely used to sharing most parts of your lives together. While that can be a beautiful thing, it is also just as essential to prioritize *your* time, space, and interests.

Retirement is a great chance to live it up with your spouse and enjoy leisure time together, but no matter what either of your visions are, it's necessary to carve out "me" time.

Start by setting realistic goals. While the first few months of retirement may seem like a honeymoon period, the luster of sleeping in together and tidying your house, closets, cabinets, and everything in between will eventually lose its new, sparkly sheen.

And once that happens, what are you going to be most excited about?

Discuss these situations. Discuss where you each want to be—together and individually. That way, you both know what the other wants, and you can use your partnership to its fullest extent and help each other along the way.

It's also important that the two of you recognize that it's important to remain social outside of your relationship, especially in retirement when you don't have coworkers to spend time with every day. For example, it may be crucial to carve out a few hours a month (at least) to grab coffee with friends, attend a class with a group, or try an activity you (individually) love. It's also a great time to discuss your overall goals for this period of life both as a couple and as individuals.

Let's say one of you wants to write a book. Maybe that partner will join a writer's group to stay on track, gain inspiration, and meet an entire community of people who share that same interest. During that same time, the other partner can find something they, too, are passionate about.

Know Where Money Fits into the Plan

Married couples need to be true partners in all aspects of their lives, including their financial situations. Once the two of you understand what the other wants for retirement, you can both plan accordingly. This sort of communication is crucial.

Do you have enough money saved to do the things you want? If not, discuss how the two of you might make up the difference.

Ask each other how much they want to spend each month. Is it the same? Is it less? Is it more? Plot a budget on paper. Make sure you're both asking questions and listening to what the other is saying to avoid confusion or misinformation from forming later down the road.

Check in with Yourself and Your Happiness in Retirement—Often

With all the changes you're experienced, one of the most crucial aspects of communication is the dialogue you maintain with yourself. Make sure that you're carrying out an emotional check-in with yourself on a routine basis. This introspective practice truly aids in ensuring your emotional well-being and contentment during this phase of your life. It can involve evaluating your emotional, physical, and social needs. Learning more about your personality type will aid in finding topics for these check-ins, but the most important thing is to routinely ask yourself one simple question: "How is this going?" and then following up with: "How can I do this better?"

Keep in mind that we live so much of our day outside of ourselves. To wit, we engage in conversations with others almost constantly, and it seems like our daily duties never cease. This is true even in retirement. It doesn't matter if we are at home, at the grocery store, walking down the street, or scrolling on social media. There is always something to distract us from ourselves. Our mental spaces are almost always occupied.

While it can feel that spending time with yourself is just another task on your mile-long to-do list, it is still an essential part of taking care of your overall health. So just as you would exercise your body, it's important that you internally communicate with yourself and do an emotional check-in on a regular basis.

Treat this time just as you would exercising your physical body because keep in mind that your mental body is just as important to your life.

How to Check in with Yourself

So, you've likely heard of emotional check-ins in relationships. But, how do you have a check-in with yourself? First off, you need to carve out time every week to ask yourself how you're doing. Retirement comes with its own challenges, and as you journey through life, there will be ups and downs. Checking in with yourself throughout your retirement is essential so you can get ahead of any potential struggles/issues before they become problematic.

This is a space where you can sort out your emotions, assess your physical and emotional needs, and make a plan for how to move forward.

- **Dedicate Self-Reflection Time:**

Choose a time of day when you are least likely to be interrupted or become distracted.

- **Set the Mood**

Turn on a calming playlist and create a space with lighting that is comfortable and allows you to focus.

- **Journal**

This is a great tool for self-reflection and doing an emotional check-in. This helps gauge how you're doing from check-in to check-in and make solid plans moving forward. This is often a great resource in show you what has worked in the past, or what you may need to improve upon. If you express yourself best through writing, or if you're the type to make tangible lists, make sure that you grab your notebook and set aside a quick little writing session. Set a timer and let it rip! You may be surprised to see what's jotted down at the end of the time period.

- **Meditate**

Sometimes the best way to really communicate with yourself is by being mindful and using a meditation technique. Mindfulness is all about using techniques to become aware of your emotions.

Catch Up with Friends and Share Your Journey

Retirement often provides a golden opportunity to reconnect and strengthen bonds with friends. While work may limit socializing time, retirement opens more doors to spend quality time with people you cherish the most. Rekindling these connections can bring immense joy and a sense of fulfillment during this new phase of life.

Sharing your retirement journey with friends can be enlightening and rewarding, especially if they're in the same season of life as you. Discussing plans, experiences, and aspirations—and maybe even taking a trip together—can create a supportive network that you need more than ever in retirement.

It's a chance not just to catch up but also to seek advice, swap stories, and potentially embark on new endeavors together. If you are fortunate enough to have good friends, make sure you're communicating with them and sharing your journey!

You never know how much you may need their advice and vice versa. Engaging with friends in retirement not only offers companionship but also provides fresh perspectives. Whether it's exploring new hobbies, traveling, or simply relishing leisurely moments, involving friends in your retirement journey can make the experience richer and more memorable.

Respect Your Own Need for Space

Amidst the excitement of retirement, it's critical that you recognize and respect your need for personal space and individual pursuits. Communicate these with everyone who you feel needs to hear it. While newfound freedom might tempt you to fill every moment with activities and social engagements or fulfill your loved ones' every need, it's equally important to carve out time for solitude and self-reflection.

Retirement isn't just about filling time previously spent at work with more activities and commitments; it's a chance to rediscover yourself and slow down. It's about embracing moments of solitude that can allow for introspection, relaxation, and pursuing personal interests without all the external obligations you've experienced for the first several decades of your life. It's about honoring your own rhythm and preferences and making sure that others do as well.

Of course, as much as a CD might like to think, respecting your need for space doesn't imply isolation; rather, it's about finding the right balance between social interactions and personal time. Setting boundaries and communicating your desire for solitude to loved ones when you need/want it is critical in maintaining healthy and happy relationships.

Remember, this phase of life offers the freedom to choose how you spend your time. Embrace social calls, of course—but don't forget to take time for yourself and communicate that it's a need and not just a want.

Discuss Your Relationship Expectations

This goes along with some of your boundaries and definitely needs to be communicated. Understand that going from working full-time to not working at all can come with a lot of unforeseen baggage. It can even feel a little stressful for married couples, especially those who are used to a little more independence.

While you likely love and care for your spouse, the thought of spending 24 hours a day with them may seem a little overwhelming at first. Make sure to establish boundaries and expectations with them before retirement sets in. This step is equally if not more essential for couples who experience retirement at different points. If one partner is working full-time and the other isn't, understand that you will be undergoing significant changes separately.

Things to discuss:

- How household responsibilities will be divided
- How much time you want to spend together
- What activities you want to do together
- What activities you would prefer to do separately

Setting these sorts of expectations upfront is a great way to ensure that you are both on the same page when it comes to your relationship, retirement, and overall happiness. Remember, it's best to have these conversations early to avoid misunderstandings, hurt feelings, and disconnectedness, but even if you're already retired and haven't had these conversations, it may be worth delving into now.

Don't forget that there are professionals available if you need a third party to mediate.

Be Honest with Yourself

While we're on the topic of communicating, it's worth mentioning that the person you should keep communicating with first and honestly is yourself. First thing first: identify your personal needs.

- Understand your personal limits: Be truthful about your capabilities and limitations. Retirement might offer more free time, but it's essential to recognize your physical, mental, and emotional boundaries. Understanding these limits helps to set realistic goals and expectations.

- Define what will make you feel fulfilled: Reflect on what truly fulfills you. It could be pursuing hobbies, spending time with loved ones, engaging in social events, or exploring new ventures entirely. Being honest about your passions and interests will benefit yourself and others because everyone will be on the same page about where you want to spend the majority of your time.

- Financial honesty: Assess your financial situation truthfully. Retirement often involves adjustments to your income and expenses. Being honest about your financial status allows for better planning and ensures financial stability during this phase.

Recognize that change is inevitable. Maybe you have a few more limitations than you originally thought; maybe what fulfills you isn't going to be possible as often as you'd like; or maybe you don't have the budget to do all that you've dreamed you would do in retirement. Whatever the case, be honest and recognize that change is in order. Embrace that change. Accept it. And lastly, give yourself a little grace and time to figure it all out. This is a new experience; you're not going to be a pro at retirement right away.

Key Takeaways

Chapter 2: Communicate Your Retirement focuses on the importance of open communication with loved ones when it comes to your retirement plans. It emphasizes the significance of discussing potential decisions as well as "what if" scenarios with those most important to you. The two big takeaways of this section are to:

- **Address Challenges in Communication**

Acknowledging that discussing retirement plans isn't always easy due to family dynamics and differing communication styles, the chapter advises approaching these discussions sensitively. Be considerate of family members' readiness to engage in such conversations, especially when discussing topics like moving or end-of-life care.

- **Avoid Confusion Through Open Communication**

Sharing retirement plans with family helps clarify expectations and prevent misunderstandings and allows everyone to voice concerns or questions. Encouraging open dialogue can aid in addressing potential future scenarios, fostering understanding, and giving peace of mind to everyone involved.

Key discussion points include:

- Boundaries in retirement.

- Living arrangements.

- Future care wishes.

- Present health status.

- How to find important paperwork/documents.

Use active listening to hear feedback from your loved ones, but also make sure that you:

- Have patience.

- Are honest and open.

- Ask for help from professionals if needed.

It's also worth emphasizing the importance of communicating with your employer as early as possible, and that you discuss benefits and maintain positive communication during your transition into retirement. Leave on a good note!

Don't forget that it's also important that you discuss your retirement vision with your spouse and determine how they differ and how they align. Work together to align your visions. And lastly, make sure that you're honest with yourself and doing emotional check-ins with yourself regularly to decipher what is working and what could use some work. Using questions such as "How is this going?" and then following up with "How can I do this better?" can do wonders in keeping your mental wellbeing in check.

Chapter Four

Embrace a New Identity

Retirement can be an excellent way to redefine yourself, especially if you feel like your career has been a large part of how you've defined yourself for years. Look at this as an opportunity to discover more about yourself and unravel an entire world of experiences that you've been missing out on!

Eat Better

If you're retiring, you'll have a little more time on your hands to plan meals and achieve nutrition goals you may have had your entire life. It's possible that you already have good eating habits, but if you don't, what better time than in retirement when you don't have work hours to prevent you from reaching your full potential?

Nutrition is important no matter our age, but the older we get, the more it affects your overall health and longevity. In fact, there is an exorbitant amount of research that shows that your diet plays an important role in multiple categories of your overall health, such as heart, mental, and bone health. Evidence points to the fact that a proper diet decreases the risk of cancer.

Recent research by the National Institute of Health also shows that as we age, not only does our metabolism slow down, but our ability to utilize the nutrients in our foods becomes less efficient. This turns into a bit of a double-edge sword because our nutrient requirements actually increase. This leads to malnutrition in a lot of senior citizens because getting adequate nutrition becomes more and more challenging.

Healthy Eating Patterns

Eating healthy foods not only boosts your physical health but supports mental acuteness and stabilizes energy levels. A healthy diet for older adults focuses on whole foods (meaning the less processed the better). Think of foods from the earth such as fruit, vegetables, whole grains, lean meats, and dairy. Make choosing healthy foods a habit so that as you age with your retirement, you're as healthy as you can be.

Since our metabolism does change, we require fewer calories than we did when we were younger. Make sure you keep a variety of nutrient-dense, fiber-rich foods in your diet. Speak with your doctor about specific serving sizes if you need help maintaining proper nutrition.

Develop a New Routine

Whether you're in retirement or not, the best way to develop a new routine is to start each day with purpose. By putting your best foot forward and starting on a positive footing, you're setting yourself up for success.

Make intentional plans for your day each morning. Write up a schedule or just make it habitual. It's important to get up at the same time every morning, and if you want your days to change from day to day to break up monotony, make part of your routine sitting at the breakfast table and making a to-do list. Pick a couple of things you would like to accomplish that day, write it down, and do it. Keep your errands at the same time every day and your planning time at the same time and you'll have a routine that is consistent but with enough fluidity to prevent boredom.

Don't forget to schedule downtime. You have worked hard your entire life to retire. Celebrate you and your retirement! Don't get caught up in the rumble of life all over again. Slow down, take time, and enjoy yourself.

How to Find Purpose in Retirement

Part of developing a new routine is to find purpose in your retirement. When you think about your career (the one you just retired from), ask yourself what you enjoyed about it. Was it using your creativity? Was it the fact that you were able to problem-solve? Was it the teamwork or daily interaction?

Figuring out what you liked most about your career can help you find something that gives you purpose in retirement and sparks a new light inside of you. By asking yourself a few questions, you may be able to figure out what you value the most.

- What type of activities did you enjoy as a kid?
- Do you like doing something on your own, or would you rather be part of a group?
- Do you enjoy being indoors or outdoors?
- If you were in a bookstore, which section would you go to first?
- Is there a particular cause that attracts you? Environmental? Animal rights?
- Is there a skill you always wished you had?

Another step toward finding your purpose after retirement is trying new things, even something you hadn't considered before.

Learn Who You Are Without Work

It's not uncommon for people to not know who they are without their job. It's possible you have done that job for many, many years. In fact, a lot of people look to their jobs for their self-worth. It's only natural that when that aspect of your life changes, you find yourself a little in want of purpose and fulfillment.

Look at all of this as a unique opportunity to get to know yourself or even relearn who you were before you allowed your job to become your identity. Take retirement as a gift that gives you time to sample new things and step out of your comfort zone. If you really want to run a marathon and work was what was holding you back, hit that pavement and get to work! You have lots of time for trial and error—the rest of your life, in fact.

Explore, be creative, and try things you've never thought possible. Be deliberate and honest about what you're willing to do. Just get out there and discover who you are and who you can be.

Keep Active

Staying active in retirement keeps you healthy and ready to take on many more years. If you're going to embrace a new identity, it may as well be one that is healthy and active!

Keep it Physical

Ah, retirement. Chances are you have worked incredibly hard to get to this chapter of your life. All those days of getting up early day after day to go to work and raise a family. Going through the rigid waves of everyday life just to be what you deem "successful" has finally come to an end. Now you can look forward to a time when your responsibilities are lower than since you started adulthood. It may seem like the end—but it isn't. It's just the beginning.

It's a new way of life, and as you develop a new routine and embrace this new identity, you will learn that you definitely still have responsibilities—but this time they are regulated completely by you. Not your job. Not your boss.

You. (And maybe your spouse.)

A lot of retirees, though, quickly feel that retirement isn't all that it's cracked up to be and become bored. With boredom can come health decline—and potentially a whole heap of depression.

It's important to note that being as healthy as possible is a priority, and in order to sustain that, you must keep an active mind and body. An active body and mind are the best gifts you can give yourself (and your loved ones) during your retirement years.

Walking and Hiking

Walking is great exercise, but it's also a wonderful activity that can allow you to meditate and self-reflect. Learn to enjoy the beauty around you with a nice brisk walk around your neighborhood, or maybe take a hike at a local park or trailhead. This can also be a great time to discover new music or a podcast if you take your headphones with you!

Swimming

Another way to start small is to take up swimming. If you love water, this would be a great choice, but it's also great for almost anyone. Bad joints, backs, etc., usually aren't affected in water sports, and it's some of the best cardio in existence. It's also incredibly accessible even if you don't have a pool. Check out a local gym for:

- Open swim

- Lap swim

- Aquatic fitness classes

- Senior swim lesson

Gardening and Yard Work

Retirement is a great time to plant a garden or spruce up your flowerbeds. Preparing the soil, planting, pulling weeds, and watering everything is a great way to sneak in daily physical activity. Plus it gets you out in the sun, which gives plenty of other health benefits. Besides, you're not only getting exercise; you're enhancing the look of your yard or harvesting fresh vegetables as a result.

Golfing

Ah, the notorious retiree sport. Golfing is a great way to stay active. Schedule a friendly golf game once a week with friends (or alone if you want to unwind). A leisurely game of golf is not only good exercise (especially if you walk the holes instead of driving your cart); it is also good for your soul if it's something you're passionate about. Sunshine, fresh air, friends (or solitude), and a little competition—whether against a friend or your previous record—you just can't beat it!

Yoga and Exercise Classes

Participating in an organized exercise class such as yoga or Zumba can be just what you need to keep good cardio going or re-center yourself. If it's something you haven't ever done before, don't be anxious. These types of classes offer exercises that can be modified so that everyone can participate at their own level.

Don't Overdo It

While keeping up with your health and physical well-being is crucial, especially in retirement when it can become easy to lose control over eating habits (whether out of boredom or another reason) as well as slow down physically, it is important to remember not to overdo it. Many retirees set out with grand, overly ambitious plans to exercise every single day or do something to stay physically fit that they may not have ever done before. However, it is important to do things at a pace you are comfortable with. First off, if it isn't in your routine already, developing a new routine may b e difficult. Start small and work your way up slowly.

Exercise, a balanced diet, and healthy choices can all be part of your wellness plan; but it's important to note that baby steps are essential if you aren't used to doing all of these at once. Even something like a weekly golf game can be enough to stay active—or going for a walk around the neighborhood.

Whatever the case, and whatever pace you feel comfortable with, it's important to know that when you make a plan, it should be something that you are able to sustain for the long-term. Many retirees find that they are just as sedentary after retirement, or even more so, despite having any established plan in place for themselves before they actually take that plunge into retirement.

Remember that practice makes perfect, and slow intentional changes are all that matter in terms of your health. You don't want to go crazy on a new fitness journey and wear yourself out at the start, either. This can not only lead to burnout but to an injury if you aren't careful. Safety measures and certain precautions (like speaking with a healthcare provider) are often critical first-steps if you find yourself making drastic lifestyle changes in terms of your physical fitness. It's also important to note that proper rest and a good night's sleep are crucial for both mental and physical health. Your body needs rest and depriving it of that rest can be detrimental to your health.

Kick the Bad Habits

It's also never too late to kick bad habits to the curb. Smoking and excessively drinking are not good for your body and can easily get even more out of hand in retirement when you find yourself bored. Many retirees report an increase in smoking and drinking due to a change in their social habits. Social drinking (and smoking) is common, and it's important that you keep tabs on the amount of alcohol you are consuming. This is especially true if you take medications.

Physically Health Doesn't Mean Grueling Exercise

Remember that keeping yourself healthy and physically fit absolutely doesn't have to mean a grueling and overly exhausting workout regimen that you complete day in and day out. All it takes is a little thought of your body's needs, planning ahead, and the willingness to keep growing, developing, and working toward a better you.

Keep Your Mental Game Strong

Getting older comes with its challenges, but you have a great opportunity to stay ahead of the game by keeping your physical and mental health a priority. Keeping your mental game strong promotes all-around good health. Not only will you feel more positive and grounded to do more physically, but you'll be able to keep your memory sharp and have a higher quality of life.

Play Games: Games come in all shapes and sizes. There are card games, dice games, board games, video games, word games—the list goes on and on. The best part? Every one of them can be used to get those cognitive wheels turning. You'll get bonus points for playing games with your family and friends, as this can be a fun way to spend an afternoon/evening and also could provide a great bonding experience.

Reading

We heard it growing up, and it will remain true: reading is a great way to keep your brain moving. It's entirely possible that working long hours prevented you from diving into that novel that's been sitting on the shelf collecting dust. That little bookstore pick that you swore you'd get to when the time was right likely hasn't been cracked open, and if that's true, what better time is there to dive into it now that you're retired?

Consider taking weekly or monthly visits to the library or bookstore and reading something new. If you want to make a social engagement out of it (if you're an MY) think about joining or starting a book club.

Reading in retirement not only offers an enjoyable pastime but also brings with it a multitude of benefits for the mind and soul. Engaging with a variety of genres, from fiction and biographies to science and history, broadens your horizons and keeps your cognitive abilities razor-sharp. This mental stimulation is crucial in retirement, as it helps in maintaining memory and enhancing analytical skills. Regular reading has been shown to improve brain connectivity, increasing both comprehension and empathy. The latter is particularly beneficial, as it allows you to connect with diverse perspectives and experiences, enhancing your emotional intelligence.

Moreover, reading can be a source of great comfort and stress relief. Diving into a good book allows you to escape the everyday and immerse yourself in different worlds and stories. This form of escapism is a healthy way to manage the stresses of life, providing a sense of peace and tranquility. It can be especially beneficial for retirees who might be adjusting to a slower pace of life or looking for new ways to fill their days.

In addition to personal growth, reading can also facilitate social engagement. Joining a book club or participating in library events can connect you with like-minded individuals, fostering new friendships and discussions. These social interactions are invaluable in retirement, offering a sense of community and belonging. Furthermore, sharing insights and perspectives on different books can be intellectually stimulating and emotionally rewarding.

In essence, reading is more than just a hobby; it's a tool for continuous personal development and a gateway to a more fulfilling retirement. Whether it's exploring new subjects, connecting with others, or simply enjoying the pleasure of a good story, the world of books has endless possibilities to enrich your retired life.

Puzzles

This goes along with games. Puzzles are a great way to keep our brains going and are as time-consuming as you want them to be. You can leave a puzzle out on the table and add a piece or two as you walk past it if you do not want to jump into a big-time commitment, or you can dive right in and put together the entire thing without getting up.

It's up to you. Make it a fun night in for you and your partner if either of you feel the need for a quiet recharge.

Write

You should be proud of your experiences and your perspective. No one else sees the world like you do. Use that. Write it down. Write your feelings.

Write your thoughts. It doesn't have to be a novel; just consider writing things down. They can be private or not so private.

Think how amazing it would be for your grandchildren to read of your experiences through your own eyes when they get older. Wouldn't you have loved to read about your grandparents? In fact, consider writing down your favorite recipes or tips/tricks. It's quite possible someone would love to read that one day.

Beyond journals or novels, though, you could also write letters. Write letters to friends, family, and your spouse. It doesn't have to be a lost art.

Make New Memories

It's great to remember good times, but it's even more wonderful to use retirement as an opportunity to make new memories you can hold onto for the rest of your life. Face it, when you worked, you likely didn't have as much time to enjoy things as you might have liked. Now, though, in retirement, there's no excuse!

All too often, many of our interests and hobbies take a back seat during our working years out of necessity. Maybe we don't get to go out with our partner as often as we wanted to; we didn't get to take that cruise; we didn't join that club. In retirement, though, you're offered the opportunity to reconnect with things you might have enjoyed previously or even connect with things you've never gotten the chance to experience. It doesn't matter what you're passionate about—you should be able to find something to try to make new memories, whether that be alone or with those you love and care about the most.

Delve into New Hobbies

As you're making new memories, consider delving into some new hobbies. Take your newfound free time to explore your interests, try something new, and spend time doing what you enjoy. You've earned it!

While it may be difficult to find what you enjoy, especially if it's been awhile since you've tried something new, trying to find new hobbies is a great way for older adults to get involved, challenge their minds, and maybe for you MYs to meet new people. Not to mention hobbies also benefit your overall health and wellbeing!

Fill your schedule with things that bring you joy, because that is the best way to make the most of your retirement. There is absolutely no shortage of interesting hobbies to try, no matter where you are physically.

Explore a New Class

Keeping your brain active is already one of our "50 Ways to Love Your Retirement," but by exploring education, you're keeping your brain active and potentially embarking on a new hobby. Your retirement is the perfect time to expand your horizons. This could be anything you want! A writing course! A cooking class! Anything!

Start Blogging

If you enjoy writing and want to talk about a specific subject, think about running a blog. It's kind of like journaling, but you have the potential to grow an audience (which can grow some side income if you really find your niche).

Create a Social Media Account

Many seniors enjoy using social media. You could start a TikTok account, YouTube channel, or Facebook page. After you choose what your favorite medium is, it could be time to get creative! Make it whatever you want! Keep up with current news or trends, give advice, or share recipes or sports reels. Whatever you find interesting, post about it. Joining groups or following certain pages/accounts is also a great way to get connected to other people who enjoy the same things.

Learn a Language

Maybe there's a language you have always found fascinating, one you need to brush up on, or one you would like to learn to visit somewhere it's spoken! Whatever the case, you can use your retirement to learn a language.

You can learn languages in traditional in-person classes or through online courses or apps. Bonus points: have a friend or your partner do it with you!

Bird Watch

Birds are beautiful. It may sound cliche, but there really is something serene about watching nature, and bird watching is something you can do anywhere! You can use a telescope, binoculars, or even just the naked eye. You can put out feeders or even join the birds in their natural habitats. This is an especially great option for a CD or someone who loves a little reflection time and peace and quiet.

Listen to Podcasts

There are an unlimited number of podcasts available for free. It is great entertainment that can be had anywhere. Whatever you are interested in, it's available in podcast form. From motivational content to religious devotionals, mysteries, sports, family, murder, alien abduction—you name it, there's a podcast for it. Throw on some headphones and enjoy; it may be the fun time you're looking for!

Join or Start Clubs

If you're an MY, you may feel a little out of touch in retirement. It's possible you're not getting as much social interaction as you would prefer. Try getting in touch with old friends, but also try to make new ones! Joining or starting a club can be a great way to do that. Let's face it, as we get older, people change; schedules and health issues can get in the way. However, having friends is crucial to maintaining good health. Joining clubs is a great way to easily and naturally connect with other people who have similar interests.

Examples of clubs you might find in your community may include:

- Book clubs
- Walking clubs
- Church groups
- Charity organizations
- Golf/country clubs

Clubs meet regularly, and people join often. It can be a great way to meet people. If your old friends aren't busy, ask them to join you.

Give Back to the Community

When you're free of work, you not only have time for yourself but you also have time for others. Giving back is a great way to socialize for MYs, but also a great way to stay active without spending money while helping people in the community.

You can learn new skills and build friendships at the same time. A bonus to volunteering is that it is really any level of commitment you want. It can range from a few hours a month or quarter to days at a time. Make sure you're balancing your life outside of volunteering to avoid burnout, though. The point is to find several things to break up the monotony and expand your horizons, not to get another full-time job.

Here are some things to consider when choosing where you should volunteer.

- **Types of volunteer opportunities for seniors specifically:** You're not in this to break your back. Make sure that whatever you're doing is for all ages or is empathetic to you as you age.

- **Finding the right opportunity may take time:** Let's face it, not everything is for everyone. It may take a while to find exactly what we feel passionate about or what fits! Explore and enjoy yourself along the way.

- **How it fits into your schedule:** You don't want to find something that takes you away from your family or the other things that mean a lot to you. It is entirely possible to volunteer and have a life outside of that. Find opportunities that fit your schedule!

An easy starting point might be to ask local organizations that you frequent if they have any needs. Museums, animal shelters, churches, etc., all have opportunities for you.

Travel More

Retirement opens the door to an entire world. If you have always dreamed of travel and exploration, and you've budgeted for it, this is your time. Whether it's a cross-country road trip, an exotic tour somewhere tropical, or immersing yourself in a whole new culture, exploring the world will create powerful memories. In fact, that is the dream of many Americans. Research shows that most Americans dream that their retirement years will include the travel they either didn't have time or couldn't afford when they were younger.

Take up New Projects

Retirement offers an excellent opportunity to delve into hobbies and projects that provide a sense of fulfillment and keep one mentally and physically active. Here are several engaging projects to consider.

- **Project Cars**

Restoring or working on classic cars can be rewarding. Whether it's refurbishing an old vehicle, customizing it, or participating in local car shows, this hobby combines mechanical skill with a passion for automobiles.

- **DIY Building and Carpentry**

Building furniture, constructing small structures like birdhouses and garden sheds, or full-on home renovation projects can be immensely gratifying. It allows retirees to use their creativity, learn new skills, and see tangible results.

- **Model-Making**

Building intricate scale models of cars, planes, ships, or other subjects is a meticulous yet fulfilling hobby. Just like puzzles, you can commit as much time as you'd like. Throw it into your routine and do it for a few minutes every day or work on it for hours. It encourages attention to detail and patience, and both can be great for your mental health.

- **Art**

Exploring artistic endeavors like painting, sculpting, or photography can provide a creative outlet and an avenue for self-expression.

Key Takeaways

Chapter 3: Embrace a New Identity delves into the transition from a career-oriented life to a fulfilling retirement by exploring various ways to redefine yourself and discover new experiences. It's important to understand that your career did not define you then, and it doesn't define you now! We visited an expanse of ways to expand your identity.

- **Improving Eating Habits**

Retirement provides the time to focus on nutrition, which promotes better health outcomes and longevity.

- **Developing New Routines**

Establishing a purposeful daily routine helps maintain consistency and purpose, including intentional planning, setting goals, and ensuring time for relaxation and enjoyment.

- **Enhancing Mental Clarity**

Keeping your mind sharp through engaging in activities like playing games, reading, solving puzzles, writing, and learning new skills contributes to a positive and fulfilling retired life.

- **Creating New Memories and New Hobbies**

  - Retirement opens doors to explore. This means hobbies or projects you love, or maybe those you've not even tried yet. It also means exploring to engage in social activities such as joining clubs, volunteering, etc. Whatever the case, enjoy the journey and expand your knowledge in any way that you can.

This chapter underscores the significance of embracing change and redefining yourself in your retirement. Become the new and improved version of who you were and who you were meant to become your entire life. Explore diverse interests and cultivate a vibrant and purposeful lifestyle centered around personal growth, wellness, social engagement, and meaningful activities.

Chapter Five

Celebrate Your Past

This chapter invites you on a reflective journey to embrace your past. It underscores the significance of acknowledging and cherishing the experiences, accomplishments, and relationships that have shaped your story up until this point. Doing so will help you in retirement because you'll be able to look back positively and know what it was all for! This chapter advocates embracing nostalgia, recounting fond memories, and finding joy in reminiscing on the "good ol' days."

Stay in Contact with Old Friends

Most of us never really think about our work friends and what might happen when we retire. Often, we're surprised that we're just not in as much contact with them as we used to be. This can hurt if you perceive them as true friends. However, keeping workplace friends after retirement takes effort. It's important to decide who you would like to keep in touch with, express that, and then follow up! Get together for lunch or text each other.

Do this with all your friends, in fact, even the ones that don't require as much work. Forge friendships that last the rest of your lifetimes by putting in the work with your old buddies (work or otherwise).

Keep Close with Your Children (But Not Too Close)

If you have children, it's important to use the time in your retirement to get closer to them. Celebrate the past you have with them but be careful; it's important not to get too swept away in that. Although it is important to get closer to your children when you have a little more time on your hands, it's equally important to understand that like you when you were younger, your children are likely very busy. Don't put too much stock into spending endless hours with your children. Instead, make an intentional effort and communicate your desire to see them. Try to plan things with them on a timetable that's good for them as well.

Many retirees consider moving from their homes to be closer to their children and their families. The question is, is that a wise decision? It is crucial that you recognize what is right for you and your family as a whole. Families used to live geographically close, but nowadays it is more common for families to be spread out across hundreds of miles.

It's very possible that you feel yourself to be in this boat; that your family is just too spread out. Maybe you have considered moving as a way to combat that. You've done your best to keep in touch, but it's just not been the same as living near them. You may be a grandparent, and you feel like some of your grandchildren are already as tall as you and you don't know them as well as you would like to. It's natural to wonder if moving is the best option. Maybe it is, but before you make that decision, consider the following questions:

- Have you talked things over (in complete honesty) with your partner and the family you want to move closer to?

- Do you really want to uproot and move closer to them?

- Do you know if they want you to move closer?

- For CDs: Would you be able to put yourself out there enough to make new friends now that you're not working?

- If your children are on board with you moving closer, what about their partners?

It's important to know that if you move, there may be drawbacks. Even if you have discussed and considered the factors above, there are still some "what if" scenarios you may want to make sure that you abide by.

What if they don't have time for you? Remember, their life is probably a balancing act right now, much like yours was when you were their age. They are responsible for a lot of things, and there are likely a lot of people who also want their time and attention. Their schedule may be pretty full. So just make sure that if you do move, you're not relying only on your relationship with them for the move to be a fulfilling and happy one.

What if your expectations and theirs don't align? You likely have expectations about the help you would like from them as you get older, and they may even have expectations on how you'll be in their life, too. In fact, they could want you to watch the kids every weekend. Make sure that these expectations align before jumping into a move. Make sure you are both comfortable with the amount of help that the other may want.

Another important step in making sure your expectations align is making sure your "why" aligns with something realistic. Why do you want to move closer to them? Is it because you want to see them more? Do you want to always be at the grandkids' birthday parties or ballgames?

Make sure that the role you want to play in your child's (and their children's) lives aligns with the role *they want* you to play. Make sure that you're also asking, "What if I have a health scare?" or "What if my child wants to relocate after I've moved?"

Answer those questions and make sure you have a gameplan in mind just in case.

Test It Out

As the title of this section says, making sure you remain close to your children is important, but it's equally important that you don't try and get *too* close. Too close means too close for anyone's comfort. It's important to take all decisions seriously rather than getting wrapped up in the romance of the way it seems in a daydream.

Of course, some families are very happy together, and the choice to be close to one another is one hundred percent the correct move. However, the opposite is also true. You need to dive into your own family to determine what is best for you and for everyone else. To determine that, it may be beneficial to test out the moving situation.

How do you do that? There are several ways, but the best is to dive into an extended stay. Ask yourself if you would really want to live in the area that your child has chosen. Experts have suggested doing a trial run for a month or so. Don't actually move, but spend extended time with your child whether that be in their home or an Airbnb or a hotel. Regardless of where you make your home base for that time, make sure you're in the neighborhood you would be moving to.

Pay close attention to everything like weather and traffic as well as where you might attend church, join clubs, or enjoy your free time. Find out where things that you need are located, such as doctor's offices, pharmacies, and grocery stores. Remember that just because you've visited your child and loved the area when you were there doesn't mean you would like to live there full-time.

Lastly, do a cost-of-living comparison. Make sure this move will be affordable. Don't just look at housing costs, but taxes, groceries, and utilities as well. Make sure your new fixed income can accommodate the lifestyle.

Best-case scenario, you find that you love where your child lives; worst-case scenario, you've spent an entire month getting to know their area and spending time with them. So don't be afraid to test it out.

Don't Forget Who You Were Away from Work

As we mentioned briefly in the last chapter, many people find their purpose in their careers. However, that isn't always the case. Reminisce on who you were and what made you great before you even started working. Use this guide to point you back to your roots and your personality. Take up new hobbies, but never forget who you were and what made you great originally. Use that as motivation to keep discovering more and more about who you are without your career.

Remember Why You Worked Hard

Retirement isn't just about stepping away from the daily grind; it's about embracing the fruits of your labor and enjoying it. For decades, you dedicated your time, energy, and skills to your profession. You strived for success, stability, and a better life. As you embark on this new chapter of retirement, it's critical to pause, reflect, and remember why you worked so diligently all those years in the first place.

Every morning, you woke up to an alarm, and there were likely nights that were spent late at the office. Possibly even weekends. Wasn't it all for a bigger vision? You worked for a paycheck, but you also worked for a life of possibilities and experiences. It might have been to provide for your family, to create a comfortable state of being, or to chase dreams that fueled passion. Whatever the case, there was a main "why." Remember that and hold on to it as you enjoy the fruits of your labor in retirement.

Remember Old Achievements or Work Anniversaries

Take a moment to acknowledge your work- and non-work-related achievements. Of course, your career milestones still matter! Those should still be celebrated in your heart, and if there is something in particular that you did while you worked that you're proud of, by all means, reminisce and truly celebrate it. In fact, it may be worth it to even budget small amounts to take yourself out on particular anniversaries or work achievement days that you might want to remember as you continue your retirement. Understand what you have accomplished and contributed to others. You might be surprised to find that it's all much more than bullets on a resume.

Take Time to Explore Family Heritage

A great way to celebrate your past is to go further back than you or even your parents or grandparents. Looking into your genealogy is a popular hobby that has become even more popular with technology advances. This is a hobby or pastime that people of all ages can enjoy. There are multiple online tools that can help you discover everything about your family's history as well as its journey through the generations.

You may know some of your heritage, but it's entirely likely you would be surprised by some branches of the family tree. If you're wondering how to learn about your family history, start by going through family memorabilia. Gather up old photographs, letters, records, postcards, and diaries—anything with a date or location could give you some clues to the past. Ask family members what they know, pick their brains, and show them what you end up finding while you trace it all back.

Choose a Family Ancestry Website

A great way to celebrate where your family came from, especially if you're hitting a few roadblocks in your search, is to visit an ancestry website. Encourage your family members to do the same!

Take a DNA Test

If you haven't yet taken a DNA test, consider doing it to aid your research. There are many services to choose from, but depending on which you choose, you will be linked to other individuals who match and may know more about your origins than you do. 23andMe is a popular database and is best known for its health reports. The fact that it's so popular means it has quite the arsenal of DNA profiles. With that many specimens, you will likely find matches that you didn't expect.

Look Back at Old Scrapbooks

Retirement offers many invaluable opportunities, and one of those is to have the time to reconnect with the past, especially with friends who have navigated life's journeys alongside you. Dusting off old scrapbooks and flipping through the pages of cherished memories can be a heartwarming and nostalgic experience and may even open up doors you didn't expect! Sharing it with your old friends is great, but maybe there are some friends you may have forgotten about. Maybe a friend from primary school that you'd forgotten about for years—looking back on old scrapbooks may be a good opportunity to try and find them again (if that interests you).

Even if you don't want to dig up a long-lost pal, there are likely some friends you still have from the old days. Gather those companions from bygone days and take a little ride down memory lane. As you flip through carefully crafted pages, the photographs, ticket stubs, handwritten notes, and memorabilia you may have saved, know that you all may be transported back in time.

Revisiting positive memories evokes laughter and joy. Relish those moments and set aside time for them! You may find photographs of memories nearly forgotten. Recounting these with loved ones is a great chance to relive stories and adventures that shaped you into who you are today.

Host Reunions

Hosting reunions from old clubs, organizations, or even schools you've attended can be a great way to celebrate your past. Of course, you could just arrange a small gathering to celebrate those memories. You could make it small and forget about it—but if you want to do something truly remarkable, go all out! Invite as many people as you can to the reunion and make it a point to celebrate it all for real. Get a list of all the people from the club or your graduating class (whoever the reunion is for) and start inviting them. What better chance do you all have to come together than now that you're all ready to retire? Ten- or fifteen-year class reunions can feel hectic because you have to juggle kids and work. Now that you're all creeping up on retirement age, consider going all out on a huge celebration. Make sure you remember:

- Food

- Drinks (alcoholic or non-alcoholic)

- Decorations

- Location
- Gifts
- Guests
- Favors
- Cake!

Revisit Places of Significance

Revisiting places that are important to you is often an emotional experience and can be good medicine for your soul.

These places are part of your life—maybe even your life with your loved ones—and revisiting them reinforces the idea that you've truly built something meaningful over time. Reliving positive experiences can be beneficial to your mental health, so make the most of revisiting.

- **Plan with Others**

Discuss which places hold the most meaning for your loved ones (specifically your partner if you have one and want to retire together). It could be the place where you first met or fell in love; where you had your first family vacation or getaway after you got married or had kids; your childhood town; a baseball field you grew up going to; or anything else that holds significance to you or your loved ones.

- **Schedule Visits**

Make plans to visit these kinds of places periodically. You can schedule a day trip or weekend getaway to spend quality time there. Consider making these sorts of revisits part of an anniversary tradition or ritual.

- **Create New Memories**

Don't always rely on your nostalgia to get you through. When you go back to this special place, make sure to create new memories there. This keeps things fun and exciting.

- **Share Reflections**

Talk about the feelings and memories associated with these places, especially when you're with another person. This is a great bonding exercise and keeps you remembering why you visited these places in the first place.

- **Stay Present**

While revisiting, stay present in the moment. Put away your cell phone and focus on the moment.

Write Letters of Appreciation to Yourself and Others Who Inspired You

There are many reasons to show appreciation for someone during your retirement from the time you make the plans to pulling the trigger and thereafter. You might want to say "thank you" to your boss or coworkers or thank a client for their longevity with you. You may want to thank mentors or friends and family for supporting you.

Sending someone an appreciation letter is a great way to show thanks and maintain strong relationships. It's extra effort that you're putting into saying 'thanks" rather than just texting it. In a digitally driven age, writing an old-fashioned letter is sometimes a nice change of pace. Make sure to do this periodically for yourself, too. There are a lot of people you can write letters to, but you have done just as much for yourself as anyone else! Be proud of you and take time to sink it into a letter of thanks.

Key Takeaways

This chapter emphasizes the importance of embracing and cherishing one's past experiences, relationships, and achievements as a means of finding fulfillment and joy in retirement. Celebrating your past is all about taking a reflective journey, and this chapter discusses the importance of maintaining those connections with the past.

It's important to remember the past with both friends and family. Get your friends together, go through scrapbooks, and celebrate reunions! Enjoy each other, especially if you're all retiring at the same time.

Family is also important in this celebration of the past. While this guide does advocate for closeness with children in retirement, it also emphasizes the need to respect their busy lives and understand that transitions have occurred. While moving to be closer to them may seem like the right choice, make sure that you're not romanticizing it and that you establish "what if" scenarios and test the waters before making commitments.

Here are a few other great ways to celebrate your past.

- **Exploring Family Heritage**

Delving into one's family history through tools like genealogy websites, DNA tests, and online resources can be informative and a lot of fun. This exploration helps to uncover hidden family stories, connections, and ancestral journeys, offering a deeper understanding of one's roots.

- **Revisiting Significant Places**

Revisiting places with sentimental value is highlighted as a way to relive positive experiences and create new memories in those same spots. Planning these visits with loved ones, scheduling them as part of traditions or rituals, and focusing on creating fresh memories during these trips is a wonderful sentiment and can establish a lasting bond to the place and the loved ones you share it with.

- **Expressing Gratitude**

There is great power in expressing appreciation by writing letters, not only to those who have influenced or supported you but also to yourself. The act of composing heartfelt letters can acknowledge personal growth, achievements, and the support you have received from others throughout the years.

Chapter Six
Celebrate Your Present

In this chapter, we discuss the importance of celebrating our present. In the rush of life, our minds often linger on unfulfilled tasks or nostalgic moments from the past, inadvertently forgetting the beauty and significance of what is going on in our present. Chapter 5, "Celebrate Your Present," invites you to pause, look around, and revel in the current moment. Hopefully, this chapter will serve as a gentle reminder that even with ambitious goals for the future or a wonderful past, there exists a huge array of accomplishments right here in the present, both big and small, deserving of acknowledgment and celebration as well.

Celebrate Your Current Achievements

As human beings, we tend to track tasks we haven't had the chance to get to or focus on the past too often. As time goes on, this can lead to a negative mindset. It is important that we take a pause, look around, and celebrate our present. The more we praise and celebrate our life as it is, the more there is to celebrate, and the more appreciative we are in the future.

Defining "Success" in Retirement

For a lot of people, success comes from achieving something. Think about it: most of your life there was quantitative measurement for your success. Grades in school when you were younger; promotions when you were older (and raises, can't forget raises!). Those external markers are almost non-existent in retirement, and we have to learn an entirely new scale to judge ourselves on.

This is where honest self-reflection comes into play. Make sure you aren't setting yourself up for failure and setting unrealistic goals. You don't want to disappoint yourself that way. Instead, set up realistic goals and learn a new way to define your successes.

Think about what drives your emotions and seems to add the most value to your life today. Who you are and where you find your true happiness will likely change as the journey of your life continues, but that's OK! You can reassess periodically. Those present-day values enable you to appreciate current successes. You may not have gotten a raise or a promotion or a shiny gold star, but to be able to look at something in your life that fills you with passion, hope, or happiness sounds pretty successful, doesn't it?

Remember, finding things that you're truly passionate about may take a little time. You have that time. Plenty of time, in fact, for trial and error. The rest of your life is made to explore, be creative, and try things you've never even considered before. But don't look to the future. Look at the now. Look at what you can change right now.

Maybe traveling hasn't been as fun as you thought it would be and you feel defeated in the now, so you're looking forward to the future when you find a new passion. How about you change something today? If you don't like trips, find out why. Is it the time that you're gone? Do you get homesick? Do you hate long hours of transportation to and from your destination? If that's the case, try multiple small trips closer to home. It's all about being deliberate and intentional. If you try to love your day, chances are you will love your day. That is because you will find at least one positive thing from your day. Petite or not, success is success!

Success Increases Motivation

Celebrating your current achievements not only makes you more appreciative of what you have and what you will continue to have in the future, but it also increases your motivation. America is a goal-oriented society, and we love being able to cross things off our to-do and bucket lists. At times, we get into the habit of measuring success with only big achievements. However, that can lead to burnout since you're too busy chasing those big accomplishments. Remember that celebrating every win can quickly prevent that—even the little ones. Acknowledging your successes fuels motivation to keep pushing forward and accomplishing things.

Success Allows You to Continue to Learn and Adapt

Retirement isn't always easy. It has its challenges, and there are times that you may have a vision for your retirement and then realize it isn't quite working out, or that you would prefer to try something different. It's important to continue learning and improving without downplaying that learning is an achievement in and of itself and equally worth celebrating. Reflect on every obstacle you have overcome. Write down what was successful and what could use some improvement. Learning from our mistakes or from what isn't working in our retirement will help us make changes and adapt.

Success Inspires Others

When you acknowledge your own achievements and what you do right in any given situation and you share that with others, it inspires them to do the same, even if they or you don't realize it. Positivity breeds positivity. Your loved ones will want to indulge in the same motivation and happiness you are experiencing. By promoting this habit, you truly will be inspiring others to celebrate their own accomplishments as well.

Success Boosts Your Confidence

When you acknowledge your own achievements, you are also acknowledging what you are good at. When you do this, you become more confident about yourself overall. And if you are confident about yourself, you'll continue to recognize that your present is something to celebrate. Remember that you can praise the great things that make you who you are. By acknowledging the goals you achieve, you show that you are deserving of celebration. Hard work and dedication mean something, and realizing your potential is key to success in retirement. The sky is the limit, and you have the potential to fly high.

Pamper Yourself

We spend years dreaming about our retirement: all the things we will do and all the time we will have to do them! We really center on those aspirations while we're still working. However, in retirement, you quickly realize that you can still fill your schedule with errands and family responsibilities. You may feel limited by a fixed income and feel financially restrained at times (just as you might have while you were working).

However, taking time for yourself will always be just as important as making time for your family and other loved ones. Deliberately set aside time for just you. Studies show that "pampering" goes a long way and can make you feel happier and more relaxed and give you a recharge to manage all the rest of life's endless to-do lists.

Relax with Reading

Sometimes unwinding with a good book is enough to set aside any worry we have with life. It can be a great escape to sweep you up and carry you away to where your troubles don't exist. Studies show that reading can reduce stress, lower heart rate, and ease muscle tension. Even if you aren't an avid reader already, it may be worth starting! It's a great time to relax, exercise your mind, and have "you" time away from the hustle and bustle life can bring.

Pour a Cup of Tea

Warm tea just soothes the soul. It can be a great pick-me-up or a nice little break to unwind. Tea can do either depending on the type and flavor you decide to enjoy. To unwind, take a drink of chamomile, which is known for its calming effect. For a pick-me-up, opt for something with a little extra caffeine. Regardless, consider using tea as a great time for "you." It becomes a fun hobby for some retirees!

Listen to Music

Music is a critical piece of art that can contribute to relaxation and set the mood for any occasion. If relaxation is what you're looking for, try soft classical music, lullabies, or instrumental music in general. Music can soothe you and make the worries of daily life wash away.

Music is a lot like reading in the sense that it has a physiological effect on our bodies. For example, studies show that pulse, heart rate, blood pressure, and stress hormones all slow or lessen when we listen to classical music. Music can really be a great way to celebrate the present because it can adhere to any mood. For some extra fun, try exploring new styles and genres periodically.

Try Meditation

You may be surprised how meditation can make you feel. Not only does it give you a great opportunity for reflection but also relaxation. Taking a class or watching a YouTube video can provide enough instruction to get a decent experience of it. Learning how to focus on breathing, posture, and mindfulness can help in other aspects of your life as well, such as calming yourself after getting upset or decompressing after a stressful day.

A beginner's class can be quite effective in teaching you techniques to improve concentration and happiness and even improve your cardiovascular and immune health.

Other ways to pamper yourself include:

- Enjoy a massage; maybe even splurge on the extra-long one!

- Get a manicure or a pedicure.

- Go to the local ice cream parlor and indulge in your favorite flavors.

- Visit your favorite restaurant and enjoy a meal. Don't forget the wine pairings if you like wine!

- Binge that TV show you enjoy.

- Go to the fancy coffee place and get your favorite.

- Have an expensive charcuterie board.

- Hit up the luxury hotel bar, splurge on a drink, and spend the night in style.

- Go to your favorite deli, order your favorite sandwich, and take it somewhere different!

- Go shopping.

- Buy the prettiest flowers at the market and make yourself a bouquet.

- Splurge on that new pair of shoes.

Ultimately, do whatever makes you happy—just make sure that you do it. Treat yourself and enjoy your retirement!

Maintain a Self-Reflection Journal

Allocating time for personal reflection and understanding enhances self-awareness and empathy. It gives proper time for a person to discover their unique needs as well as their strengths and weaknesses. Admitting personal faults to ourselves—let alone others—isn't easy. So, consider setting aside moments for self-reflection. Specialists also recommend you journal these thoughts to better understand your emotions and look back at your progress. Encourage your family members to do the same and share your insights when you're ready.

Use this personal time to explore your progress and how those advancements align with your journey in life. Self-awareness refers to a clear understanding of your own emotions, strengths, weaknesses, thoughts, and beliefs—and how they might influence your behavior, including your interactions with others. Being self-aware is fundamental for healthy relationships with yourself and others. Understanding ourselves means understanding our needs, expectations, boundaries, and communication styles. All this shapes how we interact and love our family members and friends. When we're not self-aware, blind spots in our communication and waning emotional health open the door to harmful interactions. Lacking self-awareness can lead to these and other results.

- **Poor emotional regulation**
- **Personal neglect and impaired mental health**
- **A skewed perception of reality**
- **Communication blind spots**
- **Crossing boundaries**

Being more self-aware gives us the tools to have satisfying and successful relationships. It just makes sense. Know yourself, and you'll have the foundation for a life and relationship that isn't just surviving but thriving.

Capture Moments Through Photos

Sometimes we don't remember everything as it was. Consider taking lots of photos and videos to enhance your memories and give you a tangible piece of the memory so you can cherish that as well.

Create a Gratitude Jar

Let's face it, sometimes we aren't the most appreciative of our lives as a whole. There are times we wake up in the morning on the wrong side of the bed, and all we can think about is how little sleep we got. Or we look at our to-do list and realize we don't have enough time to get halfway through it. Maybe we get turned down for a loan or we don't get to go on that trip like we wanted to.

Whatever the case, we often let our disappointments or moods affect us more than they should. Sometimes it feels like we'll never be wealthy enough or thin enough. Sometimes it feels like nothing can go right.

It's all a draining cycle.

In moments of self-defeat, remember that it's important to be grateful. Creating a gratitude jar is a great way for this! Similar to a journal, a gratitude jar is filled with little reminders of what we are grateful for. Be sure to fill those up when you're in a good mood so when you're feeling down, you can pull it out and tug out a note or two that reminds you just how wonderful your life truly is.

Key Takeaways

This chapter delved into the vital importance of embracing and celebrating the present moment. It highlights our tendency as human beings to dwell on the past or our aspirations for the future and discusses the potential negative impacts of this mindset. It's important to shift your focus to the here and now and rejoice in all your current accomplishments and blessings.

By celebrating each success, no matter how big or small, you are propelled into a world of appreciation for what your life is *now*. This is because it forces you into a mindset of winning, which allows you to foster the feeling of being fulfilled.

In fact, celebrating your present has been proven to:

- Increase motivation

- Help you learn and adapt

- Inspire others

- Boost confidence

When it feels difficult to appreciate the here and now, consider pulling notes out of a gratitude jar. If you feel you're harping on the past or situations outside of your control in a way that feels negative to your present day, hone in on these behaviors with a self-reflection journal. This will help you become more self-aware, which prevents:

- Poor emotional regulation.

- Personal neglect and impaired mental health.

- A skewed perception of reality.

- Communication blind spots.

Make sure you celebrate little self-growth wins, like when you recognize when you're being negative about something. At the end of the day, it's important to recognize that you have done very well for yourself. You're retiring! This is a huge accomplishment in and of itself, no matter the rest. Recognizing that achievement (and many others) will not only boost your motivation to keep doing good work, but it will help you learn and adapt to make changes to get even better at achieving feats next time around.

This chapter is all about loving yourself and your life now. Love yourself. Care about yourself. A little self-reflection can go a long way in not only making you more emotionally mature and better for others but also in showing how you need to care for yourself at any given time. Do you need more time alone? Do you need more social interaction? Using self-reflection can really help you uncover what your spirit needs at any given moment. Whether that be through journaling, looking through photographs by yourself, or meditating, you can become self-aware to the point where you understand exactly what you need.

Chapter Seven

Don't Forget Your Finances

Entering retirement marks a significant shift in your life—a transition from the rigors of the workforce to the freedom of pursuing personal passions. However, before you really break open the seal on the excitement of this wondrous newfound lifestyle, it's essential not to overlook the crucial aspect that sustains your future: your finances.

In Chapter 6: Don't Forget Your Finances, you are reminded of the importance of financial stability during retirement. This chapter will equip you with the tools, insights, and strategies to ensure a secure and fulfilling financial journey. Remember, it's important to be empowered, and that may be just what you need to enjoy retirement without fretting over fiscal uncertainties. However, to be empowered, you have to know where you stand financially. From budgeting wisdom to investment considerations and planning, this chapter lays out a roadmap to steer you toward financial wellness and peace of mind in your retirement years.

Get Your Finances in Order

When you're retiring (preferably even when you're about to retire) it's important that you get your finances in order. It is recommended that you speak with a financial advisor before making the plunge, but it isn't a requirement. Just make sure you have enough income to maintain a comfortable lifestyle for yourself—and your partner if you're retiring with a spouse.

Plan Your Distributions Carefully

When you think about your financial plan, it's likely that your 401(k) or IRAs will be your biggest income stream. When it is time to retire and you reach a certain age, you can start taking distributions from these accounts. Speaking with a financial advisor about when, how much, and from which accounts you'll take distributions is a crucial part of creating your retirement budget.

Plan for Health Care

We all have been feeling this for quite some time: new aches and pains. Things just don't work like they used to, and they tend to get worse the older we get. Keeping active will minimize some of these, but it's important to note that you will need good healthcare. Make sure you have a plan for insurance as well as unexpected medical expenses.

Remember Insurance When Traveling

Studies show that many Americans worry about health issues that may arise while traveling. This is because a lot of insurance doesn't cover you while traveling abroad. In fact, Medicare, the leading healthcare for retired seniors, does not cover health care or supplies while traveling overseas. However, most supplemental insurance plans do have travel emergency cover. Keep in mind, though, that these typically come with a deductible, a lot of restrictions, and a limit to what is covered.

In general, health insurance should be a major thinking/talking point before you retire. If you want to travel, make sure you prioritize decent healthcare coverage that can extend to wherever you are.

Make Financial Plans You Can Sustain

The rule of thumb is that you will need roughly 80 percent of your pre-retirement income to maintain your current lifestyle in retirement. This is likely because you should not be retiring with debt and the fact that your taxes will look a little differently.

Consider that 80 percent mark, how many years you expect to live (on average), and factor in hobbies, travel, etc. that you want to accomplish once retired. Make sure you have enough saved, or enough income every month, to do what you have envisioned for you and your partner. Make sure you factor in medical care and how much you wish to leave your children, too! Once you have done that, make sure your financial plans can sustain you throughout retirement. This will help you determine what your finances are going to look like to know if your financial plans can be sustained throughout retirement.

Learn How to Budget

As a retiree (or soon-to-be retiree) you need to know how to budget. Depending on your finances, you may need a financial advisor or accountant to look at your accounts, but in general, the first rule in budgeting is to add your income streams. These are the buckets of money that you will pull from in retirement.

Sit down with an investment professional and make a list of those streams. They can include things like:

- **Tax-advantaged retirement accounts, like a 401(k), 403(b), or Roth IRA**

These are typically the biggest income sources in retirement.

- **Social Security Benefits**

While these are great, you shouldn't completely rely on them. Remember, none of us know if those will be there forever.

- **Pensions**

While these are typically a thing of the past for many Americans, with fewer employers offering them, if you are one of the lucky ones receiving a pension from your employer, get all of the details from your HR department and calculate what it might be. These are usually based on vested years in the company, so the longer you're with the company, the larger the monthly draw you will have. Check with your company to decipher what this number will look like, and if necessary, consult with your financial advisor or accountant.

- **Part-Time Earnings**

If you decide to continue working on a part-time basis after retiring, make sure you add an average income stream for this.

- **Real Estate**

This can be a steady source of passive income if you're renting out a property that you own.

- **Annuities**

Don't forget about these products that can be used to fund your retirement.

After the total income streams are totaled, divide that number by how many years you plan to live in retirement. Obviously, this won't be exact, but you should be able to come up with a ballpark figure. From there, break down a monthly income.

Create a Zero-Based Monthly Budget

A zero-based budget helps you spend all your money on paper first, and it gives a purpose to every single dollar in that budget. Doing a budget in general will help you stay in retirement, but the zero-based budget accounts for every expense and saving.

The steps include:

- Write down your monthly income (from all sources).
- Write down your monthly expenses.
- Write down special or seasonal expenses.
- Subtract your expenses from your income to equal zero.
- Track your spending, and if you have leftover cash, invest it.

Monthly Expenses

When you're ready to list your expenses, start by reviewing your most recent bank statement. This can give you a good idea of how you spend your money. Track where your money goes each month, and make sure you're adding up all those pesky charges you may forget about (subscriptions, coffees, etc.). You may be amazed to see all the ways your money leaves your bank account.

When you track your expenses, separate them into essential, non-essential, and seasonal categories.

Essential expenses include:

- Groceries.
- Utilities.
- Home repair and maintenance.
- Transportation (gas, car maintenance).
- Clothing.
- Medical expenses.
- Pet care.
- Tithing or charitable giving.

As we stated before, there should be no debt on this list. If you are already retired with debt, discuss the best course with your financial advisor.

Nonessential expenses include:

- Travel.
- Going out to eat.
- Subscription services.
- Memberships (gym or clubs).

- Hobbies.
- Gifts.

Seasonal expenses include:

- Property taxes.
- Insurance premiums.
- Auto registration.
- Holidays and special occasions.

Use these categories as a starting point. Scan your bank account for other items not mentioned and categorize them. Have a dollar amount in mind for each monthly item.

Emergency Fund

You should always have an emergency fund. It may even be a good idea to have an allotment for that in your zero-based budget. Ideally, you should have an emergency fund in place that will cover three to six months of living expenses if a crisis were to occur.

Sinking Fund

It may be a good idea to put aside a certain amount for a sinking fund, as well. In retirement, you'll also want to maintain sinking funds to pay for things like vacations, Christmas with the family, vehicles, and recreation equipment. Consider putting this sort of thing into a high-yield account or a money market.

Manage Your Spending

Just like when you were working, it isn't enough to just set a budget and hope for the best (although some of you might relate to that at a time or two in your life). You have to stick to the budget, or it won't work! Work with your partner and hold each other accountable. If you are the type to want to splurge now and then, work that into your budget.

Remember: You're in control of this. Be intentional about the choices you make with your money. The better you stay on track, the more likely you are to hit all of your retirement goals.

Review Your Finances as Changes Occur

Remember it's important to review your finances as changes occur. These may include paying more debts off (although it isn't recommended to retire with debt, it doesn't mean that you won't take on more debt in your retirement if it fits into your budget), quitting a part-time job, selling a home, or a death in your family that takes a toll on your financial portfolio.

Celebrate Financial Wellness and Goals

Once you make a plan, make sure that you aren't forgetting to have fun! It's equally as important as being responsible. Celebrate paying off debts, hitting a saving goal, acquiring new assets, or just hitting your monthly budget.

Key Takeaways

As we conclude our exploration of financial planning for retirement, it's apparent that a secure financial foundation is the cornerstone of a rewarding and stress-free retirement journey. Chapter 6, "Don't Forget Your Finances," has directed attention toward crucial aspects like budgeting, income streams, planning, and strategies you can implement for your overall financial health in retirement.

By evaluating income, expenses, and other essential financial components, retirees are better equipped to navigate the complexities of post-career life. Having a set income may be a little daunting at first, but with the proper tools in place and an arsenal of information and plans, you'll be just as financially healthy as you were when you were working.

The chapter emphasizes the need for budgets and highlights a particular budget known as the zero-based budget, which accounts for every single dollar every month, requiring you to be intentional with your spending.

In addition to essential, non-essential, and seasonal spending, it's important to understand that other buckets also have to be accounted for. These include emergency funds for—well—emergencies, and sinking funds, which are funds for specific purposes (vacations, recreational vehicles, etc.). These are typically big-ticket sort of purchases that require a bit of saving and planning.

Ultimately, achieving financial wellness in retirement isn't just about numbers; it's about embracing control, intentionality, and responsible decision-making. Remember, your financial stability is a vital pillar that upholds the entire foundation of your retirement dreams. Celebrate reaching your goals, even the small ones, and know that you may need to adapt as needed.

Chapter Eight

Keep Yourself Busy

The journey of retirement is filled with possibilities ripe for exploration and filled with opportunities for personal growth and fulfillment. In this chapter, we delve into the art of crafting a vibrant and purposeful retirement where each day becomes a canvas for meaningful connections, personal development, and the pursuit of passions. It's all about keeping yourself busy with what moves you.

It's important to remember that embracing retirement to its fullest means exploring the avenues that life puts in your lap. You can build onto all of these with a little creativity and work. Working on your relationships, exploring new experiences, and preparing yourself for all that life brings you (the ups and the downs) is what this guide is preparing you for!

Consider a Part-Time Job

It's no secret that retired people usually need to keep busy. Consider a part-time job to do just that, and make a little extra cash. Being on a fixed income may be daunting at times, but a part-time job can help fill in financial gaps.

It may even be possible to speak with your boss (or previous boss, if you've already retired) before (or right after) you retire to see if you can transition to a part-time role as part of your retirement plan. A lot of workplaces offer transitional periods where employees can scale down their working hours over time.

Consulting and Freelance Work

Something you may have wanted when you were working was the ability to make your own schedule! Consulting and freelance work can be the best of both worlds: a completely flexible job.

It's quite possible through all those years working that you have gained quite a lot of experience in a specific niche or field. Why not use that to offer services? Freelancers and contract workers are always needed, and lending your expertise could help you and the company needing services.

Bookkeeping or Administrative Work

Another great part-time job for retirees is bookkeeping. If you are good at math and organized enough to keep good records, you could consider working as a part-time bookkeeper for a business. You do not need to be a certified accountant, though you may make more money if you are.

However, if you prefer the more organizational side of things, consider being an administrative assistant. This sort of work will keep your schedule packed with data entry and doing some of the grunt work that keeps businesses running. This would be a great fit for either an MY or a CD if they're good with calendars and spreadsheets.

Become a Tutor or a Substitute Teacher

If you love kids or helping others learn, there are a lot of opportunities to tutor or teach a class as a substitute. Being around kids is a great way to stay busy and on your toes. You can sign up on an online tutoring platform, look for local tutoring jobs at schools, or look at classifieds and job boards. You can help with an occasional assignment or an entire class. This is one of those situations that is perfect because you can choose how much time you want to commit. There are always kids out there who need a little extra help on an essay or help studying for that math test.

If you want to go further, you can check with local schools about signing up to be a substitute teacher. Different states and school districts have different requirements. Some states only require a high school diploma, while others require a Bachelor's degree or a teaching certificate of some kind. Check with the schools and your state to plan accordingly if that is something you might be interested in.

Become a Mentor or Coach

This is similar to tutoring or teaching. Many young people are looking for guidance. As someone a little older and wiser, you can offer your life and work experience to them in a mentorship. This sort of "job" allows for some flexibility and can be a great opportunity to stay busy and pick the brain of someone younger. Helping mold a young mind can be rewarding if you're ready to commit.

Coaching youth sports in your community may also be a great opportunity. If you like sports, that's even better. Doing this keeps you physically active, and you still get to use experience from your past to shape a younger generation. Check with schools or community leagues. You can potentially earn some extra money while helping younger generations.

Certain community leagues also need referees if that interests you! It may be worth looking into if you're just looking for something to keep you active for a few hours a week.

Become a Driver

In today's climate and digital age, there is more opportunity than ever to land gigs by just having a car and a driver's license. Companies like Uber and Lyft open the possibility for almost anyone to make money driving people. Cabbies are still around, but Uber and Lyft are much more common, especially outside of huge cities.

This may be a challenge for certain CDs because it does require a bit of discussion, and meeting strangers is part of the job. However, if you're not interested in dealing with strangers in your car, you can look into making deliveries instead. Companies like Shipt, Doordash, Instacart, etc., allow you to pick up groceries or prepped meals for customers. Most of the time these deliveries are contactless.

Petsit, Babysit, or Housesit

No matter what your skills, chances are you can find work watching someone's pets, kids, or even their house. Through mobile apps like Care and Rover, you can market your experience and find jobs whether you want to stay at home or go to someone else's home. Just make sure that you find a good fit!

Volunteer

Retirement opens doors to explore the joy of giving back, a sentiment that can be immensely fulfilling and purpose-driven. Volunteering during retirement isn't just an activity; it's a pathway to enriching your life and making a profound impact on your community. It offers many opportunities to engage meaningfully, contribute skills and experiences, and foster connections that resonate deeply.

- **Contributing to a cause:** Volunteering provides a chance to lend a helping hand to causes close to your heart. Whether it's dedicating time at a local animal shelter or homeless shelter, assisting in environmental cleanup drives, or just supporting local educational initiatives, retirees can choose to engage and dedicate time toward their community.

- **Utilizing skills and continual learning:** Retirees bring a wealth of experience and skills that they have gained throughout their professional lives. Volunteering offers an avenue to leverage these talents, whether it's mentoring young professionals, offering strategic advice to non-profit organizations, or sharing expertise in other ways. Volunteering provides a platform where these retirees can benefit mutually by not only sharing their experiences and expertise but gaining more insight and knowledge as well. By volunteering, you open a door to grow, adapt, and evolve through new experiences.

- **Increasing your social network:** Engaging in volunteer work can help establish new social connections. These can transcend boundaries of age, profession, or background. You're all volunteers. At a company, those at the same level as you are typically of the same job background, and most of the time similar in age. With volunteering, all bets are off. Forge new friendships with younger and older folks who share an interest (where you decided to volunteer wasn't just by accident, was it?). This sort of connection can cultivate a sense of camaraderie as well as a profound sense of belonging.

- **Strengthening mental health:** The act of volunteering has been linked to enhanced mental health and well-being. Studies have shown that contributing to others' well-being can reduce stress, boost self-esteem, and combat feelings of isolation or loneliness often associated with retirement. Add this to meeting new friends, and you have a perfect combination for a good-for-the-soul endeavor.

Find Your Passions

As this guide has stated plenty of times already, it's important to find yourself. You can do this through hobbies or other interests that you have tried—or maybe haven't tried yet and are still out there to be discovered. By trying these things, we find what our passions truly are.

Since retirement is something to look forward to and gives you a little more free time to do what you want, it's important to fill that free time with passions. They not only keep you busy but help your mental health by bringing you joy and decreasing stress.

Let's face it, saying goodbye to something you've spent a big part of your life doing can be a little scary. Retirement is the unknown! It's natural to feel a bit apprehensive. But one of the best ways to cope is to explore your hobbies in retirement.

Keep Track of Your Physical Health

Adjustments to your daily life, routines, and environment can take a toll on your health. Make sure you stay on top of it! This is a great way to keep yourself busy. If there is one thing you can obsess over, it should be your health.

Take Time to Meditate

Understanding mindfulness and meditation is foundational to fully embracing the benefits they offer at any age, especially as you get older. Mindfulness involves immersing yourself completely in the present moment without judgment and savoring experiences, emotions, and thoughts. Meditation is more of a structured practice. It trains the mind, promotes inner peace, and reduces stress through focused attention or controlled breathing techniques. These practices foster a deeper connection with yourself and your surroundings that can create a tranquil and enriched experience.

The Significance of Mindfulness and Meditation for Seniors

Everyone can enjoy the advantages of mindfulness and meditation, but retirees especially experience many benefits that aid in their pursuit of overall good health.

- **Stress Reduction**

By feeling a sense of tranquility and relaxation, you alleviate some of that stress and anxiety you have likely felt for decades.

- **Enhanced Mental Health**

Not only do you enhance your mental health by lowering your stress and anxiety, but you also increase mental clarity and your overall emotional well-being.

- **Better Sleep**

Studies show that meditation does wonders for insomnia by promoting deeper and more restful sleep patterns.

- **Heightened Focus**

This may be partially due to lowering your stress levels and having better, deeper sleep, but studies also show that people who participate in meditation have better concentration and higher memory retention.

- **Improved Physical Health**

Because your body naturally responds to calming down, you can improve your overall physical well-being and immune function by meditating.

Now that you know the benefits of mindfulness and meditation, a few suggestions on where to start.

- **Breathing Exercises**

Nice, big, deep breaths and slow exhales reduce stress and increase relaxation.

- **Body Awareness**

Mindful practice focuses on releasing tension in each body part by stabilizing your core and using beginner yoga techniques.

- **Mindful walking**

This is going at a deliberate, slow pace to engage your senses and connect with nature.

- **Journaling**

This is a purely reflective practice of mindfulness that aids in emotional processing and self-discovery.

- **Therapeutic Coloring**

Who says coloring is just for kids? This is another stress-relieving mindfulness activity. It also helps with fine motor functioning.

- **Reciting Positive Affirmations**

These are short statements that boost your self-esteem and increase your optimism.

- **Music Therapy**

As we discussed, music can be used in any mood. Certain melodies aid in stress relief and mood enhancement.

- **Mindful Reading**

This sort of reading is the same as regular reading, but the purpose is a little different. Instead of reading the book purely for the plot, engage with books with a mindset to enhance focus and reduce your stress.

Focus on Continuous Learning

Continuing to learn is essential for growth, and just because you're retired doesn't mean you should stop growing. In fact, this entire guide is about growth. Never stop growing, and never stop learning.

Human beings are naturally curious creatures. It's entirely possible that you have a degree already, but consider pursuing a certificate or degree again in your retirement just for the sake of learning. Or go back to school if you never finished and have always wanted to! It's never too late. Don't listen to anyone who says it is.

That being said, learning doesn't have to be strictly academic, either. You can opt to do soul-searching and learn things that have always appealed to you personally in a formal setting or a completely informal setting. It doesn't matter! It would still contribute to your personal growth.

Another route you may want to take is learning a vocational skill you never quite learned. Always wonder how to wire a house? Take an electrician course or learn as an apprentice. Learning opportunities in this country are immense and ready to be explored.

Don't forget TED talks, documentaries, or joining a class like martial arts or baking. The sky is the limit—the only requirement is that you fly!

Get a Pet

Introducing a furry (or scaly or slimy or prickly—whatever you feel more drawn to) friend into your life can be a rewarding decision, especially in your retirement. The companionship and love that a pet gives to you are likely unparalleled. Pets (especially dogs) are especially loyal and love unconditionally. They offer benefits beyond companionship. Their presence in your life can significantly improve your mental, emotional, and physical well-being.

In fact, the benefits of having a pet have been researched extensively, and consistently the findings indicate positive impacts on mental health. Interacting with a pet can elevate levels of oxytocin, serotonin, and dopamine, neurotransmitters associated with happiness and stress reduction. Studies have shown that pet owners often experience decreased feelings of loneliness and depression, which is great for retirees.

The simple act of petting an animal can lower blood pressure and heart rate, contributing to an overall improvement in cardiovascular health. Numerous studies confirm that pets reduce stress hormones like cortisol and alleviate symptoms of anxiety. The love and companionship a pet can provide truly gives someone (who might not otherwise feel it) a sense of purpose. They become an integral part of your support system and typically become a comfort through challenging and good times.

Responsibilities and Joys

Owning a pet comes with responsibilities that contribute to a routine (which keeps you busy). Feeding, grooming, exercising, vet visits, and providing affection and attention are essential aspects of pet care. While these duties require commitment, they also provide structure and purpose to your day, which is something many retirees feel they lack. The bond formed with a pet, the joy of teaching tricks or learning their quirks, and the laughter they bring with their antics make every responsibility worthwhile.

Choosing the Right Pet

The choice of a pet depends on your lifestyle, living situation, and preferences. Dogs offer more unconditional love and companionship and are excellent motivators for daily walks and outdoor activities. Cats, known for their independence, are great for smaller living spaces and require less direct attention—so if you want something for a smaller space that you don't have to take out on a walk, a cat could be your best bet.

Researching the right pet will take a little time and honesty on your part. How much time are you willing to commit? What do your finances allow? Pets can be very expensive and their expenses—like a child's—do not go away.

Types of pets include:

- Fish

- Birds

- Hamsters

- Guinea pigs

- Snakes

- Lizards

- Frogs

- Bunnies

- Hedgehogs

- Sugar gliders

The list is endless.

Just ensure that you are ready for the commitment that the pet you choose brings. Regardless of what you choose, each one will bring its unique charm and benefit to your life.

Start New Traditions and Celebrate the Old

You and your family likely have your own traditions. It is also possible that you or a family member may have always wanted to start a new one. Celebrate the old but don't be afraid to mix in a few new ones here and there to keep your life interesting and fun. Consider whether something another family member or friend does could benefit you. If so, fuse your ideas (and others involved) with that and try to create something completely new and tailored to you and your family.

You can even start completely from scratch and develop your own traditions on a whim. Just make sure that you're being open and accommodating, and that all of you are consistent in making these traditions true to your family.

Seek a Social Life

Contrary to what you might think or what you have been led to believe, retiring from your job doesn't have to be lonely! In fact, your social life has the opportunity to flourish after retirement. There are no more work obligations that the normal nine-to-five job places on you. You have all kinds of time to seek out others.

However, studies show that over twenty percent of adults over the age of 65 are socially isolated and feel lonely. You don't have to be one of them, though. You can easily make friends and stave off feelings of loneliness that can damage your mental health. You don't even have to be outgoing or an MY with an incredible extroverted personality. You just have to find the right groups aimed at people with your personality types! Seek out clubs or hobbies that interest you and naturally meet like-minded folks that you enjoy spending time with.

Bond with Your Spouse or Romantic Partner

Looking to add some zing or zang to your love life? Whether you are with a significant other or navigating the single life, there's always room for a little romance or a chance at love! For those in relationships, though—more specifically, marriages—why not reignite that blazing passion by spending some quality time with your beloved partner? If you are single and ready to mingle, don't worry about being retirement age! Love does not have an expiry date, and you have a lot of good years left. While finding love after 50 may feel like you're trying to decode the DaVinci code, it doesn't have to! Look at it more like an adventure.

Dive into groups and social activities that pique your interest, or consider lending a helping hand through volunteering. Who knows? You might stumble upon that special someone while broadening your post-retirement social circles. And if you are married, opt to do something like that together.

Socializing with a romantic partner is good for your health. Research shows that nurturing intimacy doesn't just help your relationship; it's a booster shot for your overall well-being and self-esteem, and it feels pretty darn good to the ego when someone reciprocates your advances.

Just because you are retiring doesn't make love's journey any less of an exciting ride. Instead of going through the motions of everyday monotony, spice things up! Learn something new by your spouse's or romantic partner's side, and open up a whole new world of vulnerabilities and newness. Embrace the unknown, support one another, and socialize in a romantic way!

Teach Your Grandkids How to Play an Instrument

If you know how to play an instrument, consider sharing it with your grandchildren. Whether you've been a music aficionado your entire life or you're just looking to dive into a new musical adventure yourself, passing on the joy of music to your grandchildren can be an enriching experience.

Remember that music has healing properties, and it also knows no age boundaries. It can act as a stress reducer and also as a stimulating exercise to enhance your memory and cognitive skills, especially when you're learning how to play it.

Beyond the mental workout, playing an instrument can truly serve as a beautiful avenue for bonding. It's a gateway to expressing emotions, sharing stories, and crafting everlasting memories.

Find Walking Buddies

Grab a friend, neighbor, or family member and take a daily walk around the block. Merely walking for 30 minutes a day can improve your mood and help prevent chronic diseases. Walking is an easy form of exercise that anyone can do, no matter their physical condition.

You could even join a local walking group or just ask around the neighborhood or at church for anyone interested in walking with you. This teaches people to hold each other accountable, and doing things with friends is a great pastime. This is also a great opportunity for people who have a little more difficulty opening up to others because it requires little talking and can be less intimidating if you join a group with people you already know. Churches are great for these. Churches today are putting a grander focus on enriching events as a way to bring members of the congregation closer.

If you're a little more outgoing, like an MY, you may be able to start this up yourself. If you are more reserved, though, feel free to discuss with your pastor (or put a note in the suggestion box) and let them find walking buddies for you!

Studies show that people who walk with others improve their physical health and enjoy a better social life. Even if you are a CD and don't love being that social butterfly, you still need social interaction to a degree. What better way than a low-conversation physical activity that benefits you emotionally and physically?

Celebrate Your Family

Even the simplest meal can serve as a celebration of family togetherness and help satiate that social need. Create memories that draw your kids home and bring your grandchildren closer to you. Initiate some new family traditions or continue ones already made. Host parties or drop in (call first) to chat and bring goodies to the grandbabies.

Another way you and your family can celebrate togetherness and check off that social box is to keep each other in the know! Add one another to your Google calendars and see what everyone is up to on any given day. Plan monthly dinners or game nights.

Reconnect With Old Friends

Seek that social life and reconnect with familiar faces. Consider chatting over the phone or catching up over a cup of joe one day. No matter how you do it—just do it! Carve out some time for them each week or each month and catch up!

Bond with Grandchildren

Not everyone is lucky enough to have grandchildren, but if you are, you likely consider it a fulfilling and unique experience. Being a grandparent comes with so many of the joys you had when you first had your baby—but this time, it comes with a lot less of the responsibilities. Being a grandparent means bending the rules a little here and there. You can skip the broccoli argument because they don't live with you, and skipping a vegetable here and there won't hurt them. But I bet you remember fighting with your kids about their broccoli back when they were kids, don't you?

There's an unwritten rule: grandparents are to spoil their grandchildren. Toys and treats are what those babies deserve, and you're going to make sure they have them!

But jokes aside, a grandparent/grandchild relationship is an incredibly important one. If you do have grandchildren, bond with them—all of them—separately. Not only is the intergenerational bond priceless, but to spend quality one-on-one time with each of them shows that you cherish and care about them. These shared moments will last a lifetime, and their positive adult attachment to you is great for their physical and mental development.

Befriend a Younger Person

When older adults befriend and mentor younger generations, remarkable benefits follow: enhanced cognitive function, improved mental and physical health, expanded social circles, and a boost in self-esteem. Plus, they may offer you a perspective that you didn't see or provide insight into something you couldn't wrap your head around before. However, it's also important to note that this kind of relationship isn't one-sided. They benefit equally from your friendship.

They can tap into your knowledge and wisdom. Studies show that there is a great impact from programs like the Big Brother/Big Sister programs. These studies reveal declines in drug use, increases in school attendance, and decreased violent behavior in program participants.

Plan a Surprise for Someone You Love

This is a great selfless way to keep yourself busy and help your social life. If you're the type of person who loves giving, or there's someone you just want to feel special, consider planning a surprise for them.

Giving gifts makes us feel good and improves relationships. Consider making this an experience rather than a tangible gift since those are generally more impactful and meaningful to your bond.

Whatever you choose to do, though, remember that it doesn't have to be a grand gesture or expensive. It could even be something as small as writing a note on a napkin in their lunchbox or stopping to get their favorite ice cream.

Remember Past Loved Ones

It may seem counterproductive to your social life to remember past loved ones. At the age you are now, you've more than likely lost someone. The first to go are usually our grandparents just because generationally that makes sense. As we get older, though, we generally lose more and more people.

It's important to remember those people. Whether they are your parents, grandparents, child, sibling, or friend, they were all an important part of your life, and their loss is something that will always be felt. Missing them will come in waves, and those waves spread wider and wider the more time that passes, but it's important to recognize them for who they were to you, especially when those waves hit.

It may seem like the best way to grieve is by keeping busy and not dwelling on the hurt, but why don't you instead keep busy remembering them? Write a letter to them and tell them how much they meant—and still mean—to you. This can aid your current relationships, too, by keeping you out of a slump and your mind on healthy, positive coping skills rather than negative ones. It's important to be positive about past loved ones to prevent becoming jaded and not wanting to interact with anyone for feelings of hopelessness.

Become an Airbnb Host

Statistics show that almost one-third of older adults live alone, and generally there's a lot of free space available in their home. If you're still spry enough to get around well and are open to the idea of opening your home to strangers, it may be worth it to become an Airbnb host. You can rent out a room or a section of your home to people.

Articles show that the average AirBnB host earns nearly an additional $1000 per month of extra income. It also provides a great opportunity to meet people of all shapes, sizes, backgrounds, and cultures!

Partner With an MY if You're a CD

You don't have to be the life of the party; just know someone who is and feed on that energy when you need a little social interaction. We all seem to know someone who knows everyone. Call them up and ask to tag along to one of their weekly game nights or outings. They will be sure to introduce you around, and if you go with someone you trust, they can help monitor your social gauge throughout the night and be a bit of a buffer.

It may be a little daunting to step out of your comfort zone, but this will keep you on your feet through retirement. Likewise, if you're a little more extroverted, like an MY, you may benefit from partnering up with a CD. They can keep you a little more grounded and help you find serenity so you're not running yourself ragged in your social calendar!

Get Involved at Church

Getting involved at church is a great way to get plugged in during retirement. You will meet people, serve people, and potentially grow in your spiritual journey.

Volunteers are always needed at church! These duties can range from Sunday school teachers to greeters to cleaners. Remember you can choose your schedule. Pick weeks or days that align with what you want for your retirement.

If you aren't religious, check out spiritual retreats and enjoy activities like yoga while you practice mindfulness and meditation.

Prepare for Ups and Downs

Retirement, like any phase of life, comes with its share of ups and downs. Preparing for these situations up front can really save your mental health as you navigate through everything.

The upsides to retirement include a lot of what we've discussed in this guide so far.

- **Freedom and Flexibility**

We discussed this previously. One of the primary perks of retirement is the freedom it offers. With no fixed schedules or work commitments, you have the flexibility to shape your days however you desire. Travel, hobbies, volunteer work, or simply leisure and relaxation become truly accessible options.

- **Finding Those Passions**

You have time to find passions like new hobbies, artistic ventures, or even time to just learn a new skill that brings you true joy.

- **Spending Time with Loved Ones**

Freedom and flexibility often grant the gift of more quality time with family and friends. It allows for deeper connections, fostering relationships, and creating lasting memories that you can hold onto for the rest of your life.

- **Reduced Stress**

Leaving behind the stressors of work life can significantly lower stress levels, contributing to improved mental and physical health. Retirement provides an environment where individuals can truly prioritize their overall well-being.

- **True Personal Growth**

Retirement allows you the opportunity to truly be who you are. You no longer have that label of whatever you did for a living all those years. This is a phase ripe for personal growth and self-discovery. Retirees can explore new facets of themselves, cultivate new perspectives, and set fresh personal goals that keep things interesting and upbeat as their journey continues.

And of course, there are also more challenging parts of this time of life.

- **Loss of Routine**

The structured routine of work life can be missed, and the sudden void might lead to feelings of purposelessness or a lack of direction. Creating a new routine or pursuing hobbies can help combat this as discussed earlier, but it's important to be prepared for it to creep up, especially if you don't feel purpose in a new routine.

- **Financial Concerns**

Transitioning from a steady income and bonuses and everything else work brings to living completely on your savings can be scary. Be prepared to feel this and plan ahead of time. As we discussed, managing finances is truly crucial.

- **Health Challenges**

Aging brings its set of health issues naturally. Dealing with health issues or having concerns about declining health can be challenging. However, having a proactive approach to health, including regular check-ups and healthy habits, can alleviate some worries.

- **Social Isolation**

The workplace often provides a social network, and retirement might lead to a sense of isolation. Finding new social circles through clubs, volunteer work, or hobbies will mitigate this feeling, but be prepared to feel it. Even if you plan on spending all your free time with your family, it's entirely possible that if they work, they won't have much more time than they did before your retirement. This happens to a lot of retirees, and they feel isolated and bored. Prepare for this and plan accordingly.

The truth of the matter is that retirement encompasses a spectrum of experiences, from exhilarating freedom to the challenges of adjusting to this brand-new phase of life. Understanding and preparing for the positive and not-so-positive can empower you to embrace retirement with resilience. Remember, you've been through a lifetime of ups and downs. Retirement will be no different. You can navigate them all if you plan a little and take everything in stride.

Key Takeaways

Chapter 7: Keep Yourself Busy is the longest chapter in this guide. It is also the most important aspect of enjoying retirement (outside of communicating your desires and needs with your loved ones). This chapter offers comprehensive insights into various avenues retirees can explore to remain engaged and fulfilled in their post-work life. It's all about keeping busy and enjoying life to its fullest.

It presents a multitude of part-time job opportunities, including transitioning into a part-time role at the workplace you have before you retire or consulting or freelance work within your given industry or niche. It also discusses bookkeeping, administrative work, tutoring, mentoring, driving for services like Uber or Lyft, and engaging in pet-sitting, babysitting, or house-sitting gigs. These opportunities put a little money in your pocket but also take up time so you don't get bored between traveling or visiting family.

This chapter also discusses the benefits of volunteering in retirement and discovering new passions. If you're not needing extra pocket change and you feel like you have played enough rounds of golf, consider volunteering or trying your hand at a new hobby or two!

Remember, there is great importance in maintaining your physical health in retirement. Mindfulness and meditation have mental health as well as physical health benefits. Areas of meditation and mindfulness that you can continue throughout your life to improve the quality of that life include:

- **Breathing exercises.**

- **Body awareness.**

- **Mind mapping.**

- **Walking.**

- **Journaling.**

- **Therapeutic coloring.**

- **Engaging with nature.**

- **Positive affirmations.**

- **Music therapy.**

- **Yoga.**

- **Stretching.**

- **Reading.**

By offering an extensive array of options from part-time work to mindfulness practices, the chapter serves as a comprehensive guide to the diverse needs and interests of retirees, ultimately encouraging an active, purposeful, and fulfilling retirement lifestyle. The chapter also suggested a variety of other ways to broaden your life.

- **Keep Learning**

Continuing to learn is essential for maintaining a growth mindset and discovering new interests. Learning doesn't have to be strictly academic, either; short courses, personal explorations, and pursuing interests formally or informally all contribute to personal growth. From academic pursuits to vocational skills or personal development, the learning opportunities are immense. Explore books, listen to TED talks, learn new languages, pick up a musical instrument, get familiar with technology, cook, or attend a class. Learn. Keep learning. And then repeat!

- **Get a Pet**

Introducing a pet into your life can bring immeasurable joy and companionship. Research confirms that pet ownership positively impacts mental health by reducing loneliness and stress and fostering a sense of purpose (which we have discussed is so difficult in retirement). Choosing the right pet based on lifestyle and preferences is crucial, but can help you feel a sense of responsibility that could be lacking in retirement.

- **Continue to Celebrate Traditions**

Celebrating and creating new traditions can put your family on a strong and solid foundation lasting after your time with them closes. Embracing both old and new traditions, ensuring openness, and consistency in nurturing the traditions will create a stronger familial bond in the long term.

- **Seek a Social Life**

Retirement presents an opportunity to enhance social interactions. Building relationships, rekindling romance, bonding with grandchildren, creating new family traditions, or reconnecting with old friends and acquaintances are ways to establish and strengthen social connections. Engaging in activities like walking, celebrating family moments, and utilizing technology to reconnect with old friends can foster a sense of community and happiness in retirement.

- **Build Relationships**

Building relationships is crucial since being social in our lives (even in retirement) is critical to our mental well-being. Human beings are social animals. We need others. Even if you're a CD and incredibly reserved, you still need people.

- **Bond with Grandchildren**

Spending individual time with each grandchild and engaging in activities they love can create lasting connections and give your grandchild positive childhood memories and attachments. This is critical to their development.

- **Strengthen Sibling Relationships**

Investing time in meaningful conversations and shared experiences with your brothers and/or sisters can deepen your original family bond. Typically speaking, your brother or sister is in the same generation as you. They are likely to be retiring around the same time as you as your friends are. Spend time with them and nurture that connection while you both have time.

- **Form Intergenerational Friendships**

Fostering friendships with younger individuals benefits both parties. Being friends with a younger person keeps you young at heart, and they can likely give insight into things you didn't know or couldn't quite wrap your head around before. Likewise, you can offer them a lifetime of wisdom and knowledge. Befriend one another and use each other's gifts to help navigate this thing we call life.

Chapter Nine
Final Thoughts

As we conclude this journey exploring the myriad ways to cultivate and nurture a wonderful retirement, it's crucial to reflect on the profound significance of this time of our life. Not only can it bring you immense joy to find yourself, but it can also be an opportunity to redefine yourself.

Acknowledge a Job Well Done

Congratulations on having the chance to make an impactful plan that can cultivate strong emotional connections with the loved ones in your life as well as the one you so desperately owe a lifetime of gratitude to: yourself. Acknowledge your hard work and recognize everything you bring to the table. Your strengths have led you to this point, and with the help of this guide, you are now armed with the knowledge to see retirement through a new lens. This lens will allow you to see your family and friends more clearly and give you the tools you need to truly grasp hold of your retirement and make the most of it.

Have Love and Compassion for Yourself

Every relationship comes with complexities, but the relationship you have with yourself is likely the most complicated. We are generally overly critical of ourselves, and why would you be any different? As we age, we become more stubborn, and sometimes we forget to give ourselves the grace that we need. Understand that it takes time to define who you are, especially if your job has always been a definer for you.

Retirement has many ups and downs, but the fact that you and your loved ones' relationships can only improve given the time you have worked so hard to give yourself (and them as a result). Use this time wisely, incorporate change, always keep learning, and understand that every person in the family can contribute something unique and impactful. Get closer to one another, and recognize that you have taken a step. Love yourself and love what you have done to get to this point. You have made retirement possible after all these years. You deserve praise and compassion from your biggest critic—yourself.

Communication Is the Biggest Factor of Happiness

Throughout this book, we've delved into the depths of understanding personality types—highlighting the contrasting traits of the Cave Dweller (CD) and the Mountain Yeller (MY). Recognizing these differences isn't merely a means of classification but a pathway toward empathy. It allows us the opportunity to comprehend and appreciate the varying perspectives that each member of our family has and shape our interactions with them.

If you take nothing else from this guidebook, remember the importance of communication. Communication emerges as the cornerstone of any thriving and healthy relationship and will aid you every step of the way in retirement. We've emphasized the importance of expressing feelings and the art of active listening.

So set clear expectations and boundaries, and above all else, show your loved ones (and yourself) that you love and appreciate them the best way you can, using this guide to help as much as you can to show it.

Embrace the Purpose of Retirement

Remember, too, that even though this guide mentions ups and downs, retirement isn't a conclusion; it's a new beginning. It's an opportunity to savor the rewards of your hard work, to relish time with loved ones, and to pursue passions you may have set aside. Embrace the freedom that retirement brings—the chance to travel, learn something new, engage in hobbies, or simply unwind and enjoy the beauty of life.

Moreover, cherish the relationships you've nurtured along the way. Your colleagues, mentors, and friends have been a part of your journey—likely just as much as some of your family has. As you step into retirement, maintain these connections but make sure you also foster new ones. Your social circle can enrich this phase of life, providing support, camaraderie, and shared experiences.

Gratitude for the Journey

Showing gratitude is the key to appreciating your achievements and the life you've created. Take time each day to express gratitude—for the opportunities you've had, the lessons you've learned, and the people who've been by your side. It's this gratitude that will infuse your retirement with contentment and a sense of fulfillment.

As you relish the joys of retirement, let the memories of your hard work serve as a reminder of your capabilities and the legacy you've built. Your dedication has paved the way for this phase of life, offering you the chance to bask in the rewards of your labor. Embrace your achievements, savor the present, and look forward to the new adventures that await you in retirement.

Chapter Ten

Appendices

Self-Assessment Questionnaire: Determine if You're a CD, MY, or Straddler

In the quest for self-understanding, recognizing one's intrinsic personality traits plays a crucial role. This self-assessment questionnaire has been carefully designed to help you discern whether you align most closely with the introspective nature of a Cave Dweller (CD), the extroverted inclinations of a Mountain Yeller (MY), or the balanced characteristics of a Straddler. By reflecting on your behaviors, preferences, and reactions in various situations, this tool aims to provide insight into your predominant personality type. Approach each question with honesty and openness, and remember, there's no right or wrong answer—just a deeper understanding of your unique self waiting to be unveiled.

Personality Indicator #1

Circle one answer per question.

1. Have you ever walked in your sleep during your adult life?

   YES or NO

2. As a teenager, did you feel comfortable expressing your feelings to one or both of your parents?

   YES or NO

3. Do you have a tendency to look directly into a person's eyes when talking to them?

   YES or NO

4. Do you feel that most people, when you first meet them, are uncritical of your appearance?

   YES or NO

5. In a group situation with people you've just met, would you feel comfortable drawing attention to yourself by initiating a conversation?

   YES or NO

6. Do you feel comfortable holding hands or hugging someone you're in a relationship with in front of other people?

   YES or NO

7. When someone talks about feeling warm physically, do you begin to feel warm also?

   YES or NO

8. Do you tend to tune out when someone is talking to you because you're anxious to come up with your side of the story?

   YES or NO

9. Do you feel that you learn better by seeing and/or reading than by hearing?

   YES or NO

10. In a new class or company meeting, do you usually feel comfortable asking questions in front of the group?

    YES or NO

11. When expressing your ideas, do you find it important to relate all the details leading up to the subject so the other person can understand it completely?

    YES or NO

12. Do you enjoy relating to children?

    YES or NO

13. Are you comfortable with your body movements when faced with unfamiliar people and circumstances?

    YES or NO

14. Do you prefer reading fiction rather than non-fiction?

    YES or NO

15. If you were to imagine sucking on a juicy lemon, would your mouth water?

    YES or NO

16. Do you feel comfortable receiving a compliment in front of other people?

    YES or NO

17. Do you feel that you're a good conversationalist?

    YES or NO

18. Do you feel comfortable when complimentary attention is drawn to your physical body?

    YES or NO

Personality Indicator #2

Circle one answer per question.

1. Have you ever awakened in the middle of the night and felt that you could not move your body and/or talk?

    YES or NO

2. As a child, did you feel you were more affected by your parents' tone of voice than by what they actually said?

    YES or NO

3. If someone you know talks about a fear that you've

experienced before, do you have a tendency to re-experience that apprehension or fear?

YES or NO

4. After having an argument with someone, do you tend to dwell on what you could or should have said?

YES or NO

5. Do you tend to occasionally tune out when someone is talking to you and therefore don't hear what's being said because your mind drifts to something totally unrelated?

YES or NO

6. Do you sometimes desire to be complimented for a job well done, but feel embarrassed or uncomfortable when complemented?

YES or NO

7. Do you often fear not being able to carry on a conversation with someone you've just met?

YES or NO

8. Do you feel self-conscious when attention is drawn to your physical body or appearance?

YES or NO

9. If you had a choice, would you rather avoid being around children most of the time?

YES or NO

10. Do you feel uptight in body movements, especially when faced with unfamiliar people or circumstances?

YES or NO

11. Do you prefer reading non-fiction rather than fiction?

YES or NO

12. If someone describes a very bitter taste, do you have difficulty experiencing the physical feeling of that bitter taste?

YES or NO

13. Do you generally feel that you see yourself less favorably than others see you?

YES or NO

14. Do you tend to feel awkward or self-conscious holding hands and/or kissing someone you're in a relationship with, in front of other people?

YES or NO

15. In a new lecture or company meeting, do you usually feel uncomfortable asking questions in front of the group?

YES or NO

16. Do you feel uneasy if someone you've just met looks you directly in the eyes when talking to you, especially if the conversation is

about you?

YES or NO

17. In a group situation with people you've just met, would you feel uncomfortable drawing attention to yourself by initiating a conversation?

YES or NO

18. If you're in a relationship or are very close to someone, do you find it difficult or embarrassing to verbalize your love for them?

YES or NO

Personality Indicator Scores

Personality Indicator #1

- Give yourself 10 points for every yes answer for questions one and two.

- Give yourself 5 points for every YES answer for questions three through eighteen.

- Write the total number at the top of #1's questionnaire.

Personality Indicator #2

- Give yourself 10 points for every yes answer for questions one and two.

- Give yourself 5 points for every YES answer for questions three through eighteen.

- Write the total number at the top of #2's questionnaire.
- Combine the total from PI 1 & 2.

Using the Scoring Chart

On the scoring chart, look up the combined score of Personality Indicators 1 & 2 on the HORIZONTAL axis of the chart and circle the number.

- Take the total score of PI #1, locate it on the VERTICAL axis of the chart, and circle the number.
- Draw a horizontal line across the page from the PI 1 score, then draw a vertical line down from the combined score.
- The number in the box where the two lines intersect represents your true, adjusted percentage personality indicator.
- Scores 61 and higher indicate a Mountain Yeller personality type.
- Scores 45 and lower indicate a Cave Dweller personality type.
- Scores 47 to 56 indicate a Straddler personality type.

Cave Dweller Tendencies

- Reserved
- Head ruled
- Controlling
- Wants space and security

- Prefers socializing one-on-one
- Singular focus
- Thinks before reacting
- Prefers showing affection privately
- Distrusts flattery
- Enjoys working alone
- Enjoys individual activities
- Wants alone time
- Dresses for comfort
- Decides after thinking about it
- Speaks literally, to the point
- Infers from what others say
- Feels emotional pain in the mind
- Fears loss of security

Cave Dweller Priorities

- Career/Financial Security
- Hobbies/Children
- Relationships/Family
- Sex/Lovers

Mountain Yeller Tendencies

- Outgoing
- Heart ruled
- Dominating
- Wants connection and touch
- Enjoys socializing in groups
- Movement focused
- Reacts spontaneously
- Comfortable with affection anytime
- Likes reassurance and compliments
- Enjoys working with people
- Enjoys team activities
- Wants to be together as much as possible
- Decides in the moment
- Speaks inferentially—adds story
- Takes literally what others say
- Feels emotional pain in body and mind
- Fears rejection

Mountain Yeller Priorities

- Relationships/Sex
- Family/Children
- Friends/Hobbies
- Career/Financial security

SCORE #1

Combined Score #1 and #2	0	5	10	15	20	25	30	35	40	45	50	55	60	65	70	75	80	85	90	95	100
50	0	10	20	30	40	50	60	70	80	90	100										
55	0	9	18	27	36	45	55	64	73	82	91	100									
60	0	8	17	25	33	42	50	58	67	75	83	92	100								
65	0	8	15	23	31	38	46	54	62	69	77	85	92	100							
70	0	7	14	21	29	36	43	50	57	64	71	79	86	93	100						
75	0	7	13	20	27	33	40	47	53	60	67	73	80	87	93	100					
80	0	6	13	19	25	31	38	44	50	56	63	69	75	81	88	94	100				
85	0	6	12	18	24	29	35	41	47	53	59	65	71	76	82	88	94	100			
90	0	6	11	17	22	28	33	39	44	50	56	61	67	72	78	83	89	94	100		
95	0	5	11	16	21	26	32	37	42	47	53	58	63	68	74	79	84	89	95	100	
100	0	5	10	15	20	25	30	35	40	45	50	55	60	65	70	75	80	85	90	95	100
105	0	5	10	14	19	24	29	33	38	43	48	52	57	62	67	71	76	81	86	90	95
110	0	5	9	14	18	23	27	32	36	41	45	50	55	59	64	68	73	77	82	86	91
115	0	4	9	13	17	22	26	30	35	39	43	48	52	57	61	65	70	74	78	83	87
120	0	4	8	13	17	21	25	29	33	38	42	46	50	54	58	63	67	71	75	79	83
125	0	4	8	12	16	20	24	28	32	36	40	44	48	52	56	60	64	68	72	76	80
130	0	4	8	12	15	19	23	27	31	35	38	42	46	50	54	58	62	65	69	73	77
135	0	4	7	11	15	19	22	26	30	33	37	41	44	48	52	56	59	63	67	70	74
140	0	4	7	11	14	18	21	25	29	32	36	39	43	46	50	54	57	61	64	68	71
145	0	3	7	10	14	17	21	24	28	31	34	38	41	45	48	52	55	59	62	66	69
150	0	3	7	10	13	17	20	23	27	30	33	37	40	43	47	50	53	57	60	63	67
155	0	3	6	10	13	16	19	23	26	29	32	35	39	42	45	48	52	55	58	61	65
160	0	3	6	9	13	16	19	22	25	28	31	34	38	41	44	47	50	53	56	59	63
165	0	3	6	9	12	15	18	21	24	27	30	33	36	39	42	45	48	52	55	58	61
170	0	3	6	9	12	15	18	21	24	26	29	32	35	38	41	44	47	50	53	56	59
175	0	3	6	9	11	14	17	20	23	26	29	31	34	37	40	43	46	49	51	54	57
180	0	3	6	8	11	14	17	19	22	25	28	31	33	36	39	42	44	47	50	53	56
185	0	3	5	8	11	14	16	19	22	24	27	30	32	35	38	41	43	46	49	51	54
190	0	3	5	8	11	13	16	18	21	24	26	29	32	34	37	39	42	45	47	50	53
195	0	3	5	8	10	13	15	18	21	23	26	28	31	33	36	38	41	44	46	49	51
200	0	3	5	8	10	13	15	18	20	23	25	28	30	33	35	38	40	43	45	48	50

About the Author

Dr. Cline lives with her husband, two daughters, two German Shepherds, and two Yorkies in the hills of North Carolina. Her expertise in relationship building has offered her the opportunity to travel around the world as a keynote speaker and international workshop facilitator.

www.ingramcontent.com/pod-product-compliance
Lightning Source LLC
Chambersburg PA
CBHW070110080526
44586CB00013B/1256